PASTA NIGHT!

PASTA NIGHT!

101 FLAVOR-PACKED WEEKNIGHT DISHES
FROM NOODLE BOWLS
TO CHEESY CASSEROLES
PLUS SALADS, SOUPS & SIDES!

Oxmoor House®

CONTENTS

WELCOME

Make tonight *Pasta Night!*

Whether you stuff it with cheese or top it with meatballs, pasta is one dish that the entire family agrees on. Simple, versatile, and oh-so-tasty, what's not to love about it? Perfect for lunch, dinner, and even breakfast, pasta stands alone or pairs well with a crisp green salad and a loaf of crusty garlic bread.

From cavatappi to tortellini, pasta comes in all sorts of fun shapes, sizes, and flavors. So if you're planning a family gathering or having a relaxed night at home, you're sure to find what you're looking for in this book. Gather around the dinner table for Fresh Vegetable Lasagna (page 123), cozy up with a bowl of Lemon, Orzo, and Meatball Soup (page 22), or go family-style with our Classic Chicken Tetrazzini (page 75). We'll even take you across the globe with Asian favorites like Pork Pad Thai (page 146).

The whole family can join in on the fun—"Little Helpers" boxes show simple ways that kids can help, whether it's stirring marinara sauce or topping everything with cheese. We'll also share our secrets for cooking perfect noodles and offer simple shortcuts so you can get dinner on the table even faster. What are you waiting for? Grab a bowl, pull up a chair, and make *Pasta Night!* your new family tradition.

Pasta Salads & Noodle Soups

Dig into comforting bowls of soup or brighten up any picnic with these delicious salads.

CHICKEN-AND-TORTELLINI SALAD

makes: 6 servings   hands-on time: 20 min.   total time: 20 min.

Prepare the chicken and the tortellini the night before to make this classic ladies lunch even quicker.

2   **(9-oz.) packages refrigerated cheese-filled tortellini**

½   **cup olive oil**

½   **cup freshly grated Parmesan cheese**

¼   **cup fresh lemon juice**

2   **garlic cloves**

1   **tsp. Worcestershire sauce**

2   **cups chopped cooked chicken**

1   **cup frozen sweet peas, thawed**

½   **cup thinly sliced green onions**

½   **cup chopped fresh flat-leaf parsley**

1. Prepare tortellini according to package directions; rinse with cold water, and drain.

2. Meanwhile, process olive oil and next 4 ingredients in a blender until smooth. Toss olive oil mixture with tortellini, chicken, and next 3 ingredients. Add table salt and freshly ground black pepper to taste.

TORTELLINI-AND-TOMATO SALAD

makes: 6 servings hands-on time: 20 min. total time: 20 min.

Baby heirloom tomatoes make this extra special but you can substitute flavorful grape tomatoes if heirloom tomatoes are out of season.

2 **(9-oz.) packages refrigerated cheese-filled tortellini**

½ **cup olive oil**

½ **cup freshly grated Parmesan cheese**

3 **Tbsp. fresh lemon juice**

2 **garlic cloves**

1 **tsp. Worcestershire sauce**

½ **tsp. table salt**

2 **cups baby heirloom tomatoes, halved**

1 **cup fresh corn kernels**

½ **cup thinly sliced green onions**

½ **cup coarsely chopped fresh basil**

1. Prepare tortellini according to package directions; rinse with cold water, and drain.

2. Meanwhile, process olive oil and next 5 ingredients in a blender until smooth. Toss olive oil mixture with tortellini, tomatoes, and next 3 ingredients. Add table salt and freshly ground black pepper to taste.

Make the dressing the night before for even faster prep.

SPEED IT UP!

BROCCOLI, GRAPE, AND PASTA SALAD

makes: 6 to 8 servings hands-on time: 25 min. total time: 3 hours, 25 min.

If short on time, purchase pre-cut bagged broccoli florets from the produce section.

½ (16-oz.) package farfalle (bow-tie) pasta

1 lb. fresh broccoli

1 cup mayonnaise

⅓ cup sugar

⅓ cup diced red onion

⅓ cup red wine vinegar

1 tsp. table salt

2 cups seedless red grapes, halved

8 cooked bacon slices, crumbled

1 cup chopped toasted pecans

1. Prepare pasta according to package directions; rinse with cold water, and drain.

2. Meanwhile, cut broccoli florets from stems, and separate florets into small pieces using tip of a paring knife. Peel away tough outer layer of stems, and finely chop stems.

3. Whisk together mayonnaise and next 4 ingredients in a large bowl; add broccoli, pasta, and grapes, and stir to coat. Cover and chill 3 hours. Stir bacon and pecans into salad just before serving.

Pasta Pointer

Cook the pasta al dente (firm to the bite) so it's firm enough to hold its own when tossed with the tangy-sweet salad dressing.

GREEN BEAN PASTA SALAD
WITH LEMON-THYME VINAIGRETTE

makes: 4 to 6 servings hands-on time: 15 min. total time: 30 min.

Casarecce [cah-sah-RECH-ee] pasta looks similar to a scroll with the long sides curled inward toward the center.

- 12 oz. uncooked casarecce pasta*
- ½ lb. haricots verts (thin green beans), cut in half lengthwise
- 1 Tbsp. fresh thyme
- 5 tsp. lemon zest, divided
- ¼ cup finely chopped, roasted, salted pistachios
- 2 Tbsp. Champagne vinegar
- 1 Tbsp. minced shallots
- 1 garlic clove, minced
- 1 tsp. table salt
- ½ tsp. freshly ground black pepper
- 5 Tbsp. olive oil
- 1½ cups loosely packed arugula

Toppings: chopped roasted, salted pistachios; shaved Parmesan cheese

1. Cook pasta according to package directions, stirring in green beans during last 2 minutes of cooking; drain. Rinse pasta mixture with cold water; drain.

2. Place pasta mixture, thyme, and 3 tsp. lemon zest in a large bowl; toss gently to combine.

3. Whisk together ¼ cup pistachios, next 5 ingredients, and remaining 2 tsp. lemon zest in a small bowl. Add oil in a slow, steady stream, whisking constantly until blended. Drizzle over pasta mixture. Add arugula, and toss gently to coat. Serve with desired toppings.

* Penne pasta may be substituted.

CREAMY SHRIMP-AND-MACARONI SALAD

makes: 4 servings   hands-on time: 20 min.   total time: 50 min.

Vigorously stir the dressing ingredients to prevent it from separating.

- 1   (8-oz.) package elbow macaroni
- ½   cup chopped celery
- ½   cup chopped green onions
- ½   cup plus 3 Tbsp. mayonnaise
- ¼   cup chopped fresh parsley
- 1   Tbsp. country-style Dijon mustard
- 1   Tbsp. chopped fresh tarragon
- 2   tsp. white wine vinegar
- 1   tsp. sugar
- ½   tsp. table salt
- ¼   tsp. freshly ground black pepper
- 1   lb. peeled Perfect Poached Shrimp

1. Prepare macaroni according to package directions; rinse with cold water, and drain. Stir together celery, green onions, mayonnaise, parsley, Dijon mustard, tarragon, vinegar, sugar, salt, and pepper.

2. Coarsely chop Perfect Poached Shrimp; stir shrimp and mayonnaise mixture into pasta. Cover and chill 1 hour.

PERFECT POACHED SHRIMP

makes: 3 to 4 servings
hands-on time: 15 min.
total time: 30 min.

- Ice
- 1   lemon, halved
- 1   Tbsp. black peppercorns
- 2   bay leaves
- 2   tsp. table salt
- 2   lb. unpeeled, large raw shrimp

1. Fill a large bowl halfway with ice and water. Pour 4 qt. water into a Dutch oven; squeeze juice from lemon into Dutch oven. Stir in lemon halves, black peppercorns, bay leaves, and salt; bring to a boil over medium-high heat. Remove from heat; add shrimp. Cover and let stand 5 minutes or just until shrimp turn pink. Stir shrimp into ice water; let stand 10 minutes. Drain. Peel and devein shrimp.

TANGY TZATZIKI PASTA SALAD

makes: 10 servings hands-on time: 35 min. total time: 2 hours, 35 min.

Pat the sun-dried tomatoes in oil well with paper towels to remove excess oil.

- 1 (16-oz.) container low-fat plain Greek yogurt
- ¼ cup olive oil
- 1 Tbsp. chopped fresh dill
- 1 Tbsp. lemon juice
- 1 tsp. sea salt
- ½ tsp. freshly ground black pepper
- 3 garlic cloves
- 1 (16-oz.) package penne pasta
- 1 cup pitted kalamata olives, sliced
- 2 cucumbers, peeled, seeded, and diced
- ¾ cup sun-dried tomatoes in oil, drained and chopped
- 1 (9.9-oz.) jar marinated artichoke hearts, drained and chopped
- 1½ cups crumbled feta cheese

1. Process first 7 ingredients in a food processor 30 seconds or until thoroughly blended. Transfer to a bowl, and cover and chill 1 to 24 hours.

2. Meanwhile, cook pasta according to package directions; rinse with cold water, and drain.

3. Place pasta in a large bowl. Stir in olives and next 3 ingredients until well blended. Add yogurt mixture, and stir just until well coated. Gently stir in feta cheese. Cover and chill 1 hour.

Pasta Pointer

Feel free to substitute gluten-free penne pasta.

CHINESE CHICKEN NOODLE BOWLS

makes: 6 servings   hands-on time: 10 min.   total time: 45 min.

Fresh lime juice adds extra bright flavor to the broth. Bringing the broth back to a boil before serving ensures the snap peas cook to a crisp-tender texture.

- **6   cups chicken broth**
- **4   skinned and boned chicken thighs (about 1 lb.)**
- **⅓   cup sliced fresh ginger**
- **2   garlic cloves, sliced**
- **⅛   tsp. Chinese five spice**
- **1   (9.5-oz.) package soba noodles or 8 oz. angel hair pasta**
- **1   Tbsp. soy sauce**
- **Toppings: fresh cilantro and mint leaves, thinly sliced green onions, thinly sliced red chile peppers**
- **2   cups sugar snap peas, sliced lengthwise**
- **2   to 3 Tbsp. fresh lime juice**

1. Bring first 5 ingredients to a boil in a 3-qt. saucepan over medium heat. Cover, reduce heat to low, and simmer 6 to 8 minutes or until chicken is done. Remove chicken, garlic, and ginger with a slotted spoon, reserving broth in saucepan. Discard garlic and ginger. Let chicken cool slightly (10 to 15 minutes); shred chicken.

2. Return broth to a boil over medium heat. Add noodles and soy sauce; cook, stirring to separate noodles, 4 to 5 minutes or until just softened. Remove noodles from broth using tongs, and divide among 6 bowls. Place chicken and desired toppings on noodles. Stir in sugar snap peas and lime juice to broth, and return to a boil over medium heat. Remove from heat, and divide broth mixture among bowls.

Shred a rotisserie chicken from the deli department. Stir in when adding the sugar snap peas.

SPEED IT UP!

FARMERS' MARKET PASTA SALAD

makes: 8 to 10 servings hands-on time: 20 min. total time: 25 min.

Cook pasta al dente (firm to the bite) so it holds its shape when tossed with the vegetables and vinaigrette. Ripe for riffs, the salad is also delicious with cheese-filled tortellini.

2	cups halved baby heirloom tomatoes	½	cup thinly sliced green onions
2	small zucchini, thinly sliced into half moons	1	(8-oz.) package penne pasta
1	small red bell pepper, cut into thin strips	2	cups shredded smoked chicken (about 10 oz.)
1	cup fresh corn kernels		**Parmesan Vinaigrette**
1	cup diced firm, ripe fresh peaches (about 2 medium)	⅓	cup torn fresh basil
		⅓	cup torn fresh cilantro

1. Toss together first 6 ingredients in a large bowl, and let stand 10 minutes.

2. Meanwhile, prepare pasta according to package directions; rinse pasta with cold water, and drain. Add pasta and chicken to tomato mixture; toss gently to coat. Drizzle Parmesan Vinaigrette over salad; toss gently. Add salt and freshly ground black pepper to taste. Transfer to a serving platter, and top with basil and cilantro.

PARMESAN VINAIGRETTE

makes: about 1 cup
hands-on time: 5 min.
total time: 5 min.

½	cup freshly grated Parmesan cheese
½	cup olive oil
2	tsp. loosely packed lemon zest
3	Tbsp. fresh lemon juice
1	Tbsp. balsamic vinegar
2	garlic cloves
2	tsp. freshly ground black pepper
½	tsp. table salt
¼	cup chopped fresh basil
¼	cup chopped fresh cilantro

1. Process Parmesan cheese, olive oil, lemon zest, lemon juice, balsamic vinegar, garlic, pepper, and salt in a blender or food processor until smooth. Add basil and cilantro; pulse 5 or 6 times or just until blended.

LEMON, ORZO, AND MEATBALL SOUP

makes: about 3 qt. hands-on time: 23 min. total time: 35 min.

This comforting soup is the Greek version of Italian wedding soup. To prevent the meatballs from becoming tough, use a gentle hand to shape them.

- 1 lb. ground chicken
- 1 large egg, lightly beaten
- ¼ cup fine, dry breadcrumbs
- 1 tsp. kosher salt
- 4 tsp. loosely packed lemon zest, divided
- 1 tsp. dried crushed rosemary, divided
- 3 Tbsp. olive oil, divided
- 1 medium-size sweet onion, chopped
- 3 carrots, thinly sliced
- 2 garlic cloves, minced
- 2 (32-oz.) containers chicken broth
- 5 to 6 Tbsp. lemon juice
- ¾ cup orzo pasta
- ¼ cup freshly grated Parmesan cheese
- ½ cup fresh flat-leaf parsley

1. Combine first 4 ingredients, 2 tsp. lemon zest, and ½ tsp. rosemary in a medium bowl. Shape into 30 (1-inch) meatballs (about 1 Tbsp. each).

2. Sauté meatballs, in 2 batches, in 1 Tbsp. hot oil per batch in a Dutch oven over medium heat 3 to 4 minutes or until browned. Remove using a slotted spoon.

3. Sauté onion and next 2 ingredients in remaining 1 Tbsp. hot oil in Dutch oven over medium-high heat 3 to 5 minutes or until tender. Stir in broth, lemon juice, and remaining 2 tsp. zest and ½ tsp. rosemary. Bring to a boil, stirring occasionally. Add orzo. Reduce heat to medium; simmer, stirring occasionally, 7 to 9 minutes or until pasta is almost tender.

4. Stir in meatballs; simmer, stirring occasionally, 5 to 7 minutes or until meatballs are thoroughly cooked. Add table salt and freshly ground black pepper to taste. Top with cheese and parsley.

THAI NOODLE SALAD

makes: 4 servings hands-on time: 25 min. total time: 25 min.

This refreshing salad is perfect for lunch or a warm summer day. Serve it with steamed edamame to round out the meal.

1   (8-oz.) package vermicelli

⅓   cup chopped fresh cilantro

2   garlic cloves, minced

1   jalapeño pepper, seeded and chopped

¼   cup fresh lime juice

1   Tbsp. fish sauce*

1   Tbsp. honey

1½ tsp. sesame oil

¼   tsp. table salt

2   carrots, grated

1   cucumber, peeled, seeded, and thinly sliced

1   cup finely shredded cabbage

¼   cup chopped fresh mint

¼   cup chopped dry-roasted peanuts

Garnish: lime slices

1. Cook pasta according to package directions; rinse with cold water, and drain.

2. Meanwhile, process cilantro and next 7 ingredients in a food processor until smooth, stopping to scrape down sides.

3. Toss together pasta, cilantro dressing, carrots, and next 3 ingredients. Sprinkle with peanuts, and serve immediately.

* Soy sauce may be substituted for fish sauce.

Use English cucumbers, which do not require peeling or seeding.

Speed It Up!

BEEFY MINESTRONE SOUP

makes: 6 servings hands-on time: 3 min. total time: 13 min.

Need dinner in a jiffy? Convenience foods such as canned broth, tomatoes, and beans get this hearty soup on the table in just 13 minutes.

⅔ cup uncooked ditalini (very short, tube-shaped macaroni)

2 (14-oz.) cans reduced-sodium fat-free beef broth

1 (14.5-oz.) can no-salt-added stewed tomatoes, undrained

1 large zucchini

1 (15.5-oz.) can cannellini beans or other white beans, drained and rinsed

2 tsp. dried Italian seasoning

8 oz. deli rare roast beef, sliced ¼ inch thick and diced

1. Combine first 3 ingredients in a large saucepan; cover and bring to a boil over high heat.

2. Cut zucchini in half lengthwise, and slice. Add zucchini, beans, and Italian seasoning to pasta; cover, reduce heat, and simmer 6 minutes. Add beef, and cook 4 minutes or until pasta is tender.

Pasta Pointer

Zucchini is abundant and inexpensive during its peak months of June through late August. Select firm, unblemished zucchini. Store zucchini in a perforated plastic bag in the refrigerator crisper drawer for up to three days.

RAMEN NOODLE SALAD

makes: 8 to 10 servings hands-on time: 10 min. total time: 15 min.

To prevent the ramen noodles from losing their crunch, assemble the salad right before serving.

1 (3-oz.) package ramen noodle soup mix

¼ cup butter

1 cup walnuts or pecans, chopped

1 (16-oz.) package fresh broccoli florets

1 head romaine lettuce, torn

4 green onions, chopped

Sweet-and-Sour Dressing

1. Remove seasoning packet from ramen noodles, and reserve for another use. Break noodles into pieces.

2. Melt butter in a large skillet over medium-high heat; add ramen noodles and walnuts, and sauté until lightly browned. Drain on paper towels.

3. Toss together noodle mixture, broccoli, lettuce, and green onions in a large bowl; add ¼ cup Sweet-and-Sour Dressing, tossing to coat. Serve with remaining dressing.

SWEET-AND-SOUR DRESSING

makes: 1 cup
hands-on time: 5 min.
total time: 5 min.

½ cup vegetable oil

¼ cup sugar

¼ cup red wine vinegar

1 Tbsp. soy sauce

½ tsp. table salt

¼ tsp. freshly ground black pepper

1. Whisk together oil and remaining ingredients.

SHRIMP AND NOODLE SALAD
WITH ASIAN VINAIGRETTE DRESSING

makes: 4 servings   hands-on time: 9 min.   total time: 14 min.

Soy, ginger, and garlic give this nutty noodle salad an extra dimension of tantalizing flavor. Look for rice noodles in the ethnic food section of your supermarket.

- 2 oz. dried rice noodles (such as Hokan)
- Asian Vinaigrette Dressing
- 4 cups thinly sliced napa cabbage
- ¾ lb. peeled large, cooked shrimp, deveined
- 1 cup snow peas, trimmed and cut diagonally in half
- 3 cups fresh bean sprouts
- 3 Tbsp. thinly sliced green onions (optional)
- ¼ cup chopped fresh cilantro (optional)

1. Cook noodles in boiling water 5 minutes; rinse with cold water. Drain.

2. Meanwhile, prepare Asian Vinaigrette Dressing.

3. Combine noodles, cabbage, and next 3 ingredients. Add dressing, and toss well. Sprinkle salad with green onions and cilantro, if desired.

ASIAN VINAIGRETTE DRESSING

makes: about ½ cup
hands-on time: 6 min.
total time: 6 min.

- 3 Tbsp. lime juice
- 1½ tsp. fish sauce
- 1½ Tbsp. creamy peanut butter
- 2 tsp. sugar
- 2 tsp. grated fresh ginger
- 2 tsp. reduced-sodium soy sauce
- 2 tsp. dark sesame oil
- 2 garlic cloves, minced

1. Whisk together all ingredients until smooth.

STEAK SOUP

makes: 6 servings   hands-on time: 15 min.   total time: 8 hours, 45 min.

2¼ lb. sirloin tip roast, cut into 1-inch cubes

¼ cup all-purpose flour

½ tsp. table salt

½ tsp. coarsely ground black pepper

2 Tbsp. canola oil

1 (1-oz.) envelope dry onion soup mix

4 cups beef broth

1 Tbsp. tomato paste

1 Tbsp. Worcestershire sauce

2 cups uncooked wide egg noodles

1. Combine first 4 ingredients in a large zip-top plastic freezer bag; seal bag, and shake to coat beef.

2. Sauté beef in hot oil in a Dutch oven over medium-high heat 6 minutes or until browned. Place in a 4-qt. slow cooker. Sprinkle onion soup mix over beef. Whisk together beef broth, tomato paste, and Worcestershire; pour over beef. Cover and cook on LOW 8 hours or until beef is tender.

3. Add noodles to slow cooker; cover and cook 30 minutes or until noodles are done.

Pasta Pointer

Sirloin tip is a leaner cut than traditional chuck roast. It yields a very tender "fall-apart" texture after the long, slow cooking.

VEGETABLE TORTELLINI SOUP

makes: 6 servings hands-on time: 5 min. total time: 7 hours, 23 min.

Serve this hearty soup with a rustic loaf of bread.

2 **(8-oz.) packages refrigerated celery, onion, and bell pepper mix**

1 **medium zucchini, coarsely chopped**

1 **(32-oz.) container chicken broth**

1 **(16-oz.) package frozen baby corn, bean, pea, and carrot mix**

1 **(15.5-oz.) can cannellini beans, drained and rinsed**

1 **(14.5-oz.) can diced tomatoes with basil, oregano, and garlic, undrained**

½ **tsp. freshly ground black pepper**

1 **(9-oz.) package refrigerated cheese-filled tortellini**

Garnish: shredded Parmesan cheese

1. Heat a large nonstick skillet over medium-high heat. Coat pan with cooking spray. Add celery mixture, and sauté 5 minutes or until tender. Transfer mixture to a 5-qt. slow cooker. Stir in zucchini and next 5 ingredients. Cover and cook on LOW for 7 hours.

2. Increase heat to HIGH; add tortellini. Cover and cook 18 minutes or until pasta is tender.

Pasta Pointer

Try substituting spinach- or chicken-filled tortellini. You can also use ravioletti (small ravioli that just fit in your spoon).

COCONUT-CURRY NOODLE SOUP

makes: 6 cups hands-on time: 10 min. total time: 20 min.

For the daring, don't remove the seeds, which is where most of a chile's heat comes from.

2 (3-oz.) packages ramen noodle soup mix

1 (14-oz.) can chicken broth

1 (14-oz.) can coconut milk

1 Thai chile or jalapeño pepper, seeded and halved

1 Tbsp. minced garlic

1 Tbsp. minced fresh ginger

1 Tbsp. curry powder

1 Tbsp. chopped fresh cilantro

1 Tbsp. chopped shallots

1. Remove seasoning packet from ramen soup mix, and reserve for another use.

2. Bring 1 qt. water to a boil in a large saucepan; add noodles, and boil 2 minutes. Rinse with cold water; drain.

3. Bring broth and next 7 ingredients to a boil in saucepan; reduce heat, and simmer 10 minutes. Remove chile pepper, and stir in noodles.

ALPHABET CHICKEN SOUP

makes: about 10 cups hands-on time: 10 min. total time: 39 min.

If you want to use homemade broth but don't have quite 8 cups, use packaged broth to make up the difference. Any small pasta will work in this recipe.

1   medium onion, chopped

2   carrots, chopped

2   celery ribs, chopped

1   Tbsp. vegetable oil

2   garlic cloves, minced

2   (32-oz.) containers chicken broth

2   cups Seasoned Shredded Chicken

¼   tsp. dried thyme

½   cup alphabet-shaped pasta, uncooked

1. Sauté first 3 ingredients in hot oil in a Dutch oven over medium-high heat 5 minutes; add garlic, and sauté 1 minute.

2. Stir in broth, chicken, thyme, and table salt and freshly ground black pepper to taste. Bring to a boil; reduce heat, and simmer, stirring occasionally, 15 minutes.

3. Stir in pasta, and cook 8 more minutes.

SEASONED SHREDDED CHICKEN

makes: about 6 cups
hands-on time: 5 min.
total time: 40 min.

6   skinless, bone-in chicken breasts

6   chicken bouillon cubes

1. Bring chicken, water to cover, and bouillon cubes to a boil over high heat in a large saucepan. Reduce heat, and simmer 20 to 25 minutes or until chicken is done. Remove chicken from broth, and cool slightly; pull meat from bones, and shred with a fork, discarding bones. Sprinkle with table salt and seasoned pepper to taste. Place in large zip-top plastic freezer bags, and freeze up to 1 month. Thaw in refrigerator overnight.

VEGETABLE SOUP
WITH BASIL PISTOU

makes: about 10 cups hands-on time: 42 min. total time: 50 min.

Pistou is similar to basil pesto but made without pine nuts.

2 carrots, chopped

2 celery ribs, chopped

1 large sweet onion, chopped

4 garlic cloves, minced

1 tsp. minced fresh thyme

1 Tbsp. olive oil

2 (32-oz.) containers organic vegetable broth

2 plum tomatoes, seeded and chopped

1 zucchini, chopped

1¼ tsp. kosher salt

½ tsp. freshly ground black pepper

1 (15.5-oz.) can cannellini beans, drained and rinsed

½ cup uncooked mini farfalle (bow-tie) pasta

Basil Pistou

1. Sauté carrots and next 4 ingredients in hot oil in a Dutch oven over medium-high heat 8 to 10 minutes or until vegetables are tender. Stir in broth, tomatoes, zucchini, salt, and pepper; bring to a boil. Reduce heat to medium-low, and simmer, stirring occasionally, 10 minutes.

2. Stir in beans and pasta, and cook, stirring occasionally, 10 to 12 minutes or until pasta is tender. Top each serving with 1 to 2 tsp. Basil Pistou.

BASIL PISTOU

makes: about ½ cup
hands-on time: 5 min.
total time: 5 min.

2 cups firmly packed fresh basil leaves

½ cup freshly grated Parmesan cheese

3 Tbsp. extra virgin olive oil

1 garlic clove, chopped

½ tsp. kosher salt

1. Process all ingredients in a food processor until finely ground. Refrigerate in an airtight container up to 1 week.

SOUTHERN ITALIAN CHICKEN SOUP

makes: 8 servings hands-on time: 45 min. total time: 50 min.

If fresh okra is not in season, substitute frozen.

1   large onion, diced

1   celery rib, thinly sliced

2   carrots, chopped

1   garlic clove, minced

3   Tbsp. olive oil, divided

6   cups chicken broth

1   (14.5-oz.) can diced tomatoes

1   tsp. dried Italian seasoning

¼   tsp. dried crushed red pepper

4   (6- to 8-oz.) skinned and boned chicken breasts

½   tsp. table salt

½   tsp. freshly ground black pepper

2   cups sliced fresh okra

1   (15.5-oz.) can black-eyed peas, drained and rinsed

1   (9-oz.) package refrigerated cheese-filled tortellini

Freshly grated Parmesan cheese

1. Sauté first 4 ingredients in 2 Tbsp. hot oil in a large Dutch oven over medium-high heat 3 to 5 minutes or until tender. Stir in broth and next 3 ingredients; bring to a boil, stirring occasionally. Reduce heat to medium, and simmer, stirring occasionally, 10 minutes.

2. Meanwhile, sprinkle chicken with salt and pepper. Cook in remaining 1 Tbsp. hot oil in a large nonstick skillet over medium-high heat 5 minutes on each side or until lightly browned. Cool slightly (about 5 minutes); cut into 1-inch pieces.

3. Add okra, black-eyed peas, and chicken to Dutch oven. Simmer, stirring occasionally, 10 minutes or until okra is tender. Add tortellini, and cook, stirring occasionally, 3 minutes or until tortellini is done. Serve with Parmesan cheese.

FAMILY FAVORITES

From mac 'n' cheese
to chicken parm,
we guarantee your dining room
table will always be filled with food
your family will love.

BAKED SMOKIN' MACARONI AND CHEESE

makes: 8 servings   hands-on time: 25 min.   total time: 1 hour

A trio of cheeses coats fun-to-eat cork-screw pasta in this take on the comfort food classic. Smoked ham adds some heft.

1	lb. uncooked cellentani (corkscrew) pasta	3	oz. fat-free cream cheese, softened
2	Tbsp. butter	½	tsp. table salt
¼	cup all-purpose flour	¼	tsp. ground red pepper, divided
3	cups fat-free milk		
1	(12-oz.) can fat-free evaporated milk	1	(8-oz.) package chopped smoked ham
1	cup (4 oz.) shredded smoked Gouda cheese	1¼	cups cornflakes cereal, crushed
½	cup (2 oz.) shredded 50% reduced-fat sharp Cheddar cheese	1	Tbsp. butter, melted

1. Preheat oven to 350°. Prepare pasta according to package directions.

2. Meanwhile, melt 2 Tbsp. butter in a Dutch oven over medium heat. Gradually whisk in flour; cook, whisking constantly, 1 minute. Gradually whisk in milk and evaporated milk until smooth; cook, whisking constantly, 8 to 10 minutes or until slightly thickened. Whisk in Gouda cheese, next 3 ingredients, and ⅛ tsp. ground red pepper until smooth. Remove from heat, and stir in ham and pasta.

3. Pour pasta mixture into a 13- x 9-inch baking dish coated with cooking spray. Stir together crushed cereal, 1 Tbsp. melted butter, and remaining ⅛ tsp. ground red pepper; sprinkle over pasta mixture.

4. Bake at 350° for 30 minutes or until golden and bubbly. Let stand 5 minutes before serving.

Note: We tested with Barilla® Cellentani pasta and Cabot® 50% Reduced Fat Sharp Cheddar Cheese.

Little Helpers

Place the cornflakes in a zip-top plastic freezer bag and let your kids crush the flakes. They'll love the crunching noise!

PAN-FRIED CHICKEN-AND-HAM PARMESAN

makes: 4 servings hands-on time: 10 min. total time: 26 min.

Serve with herbed pasta and sautéed tomatoes for an easy dinner that's perfect for company or family.

4   (6-oz.) skinned and boned chicken breasts

1   tsp. table salt

½   tsp. freshly ground black pepper

1   large egg

¼   cup all-purpose flour

⅔   cup Italian-seasoned breadcrumbs

2   Tbsp. olive oil

8   thinly sliced smoked deli ham slices (about ¼ lb.)

4   (1-oz.) fresh mozzarella cheese slices

Garlic-Herb Pasta

Sautéed Grape Tomatoes

1. Preheat oven to 350°. Sprinkle chicken with salt and pepper. Whisk together egg and 2 Tbsp. water. Dredge chicken in flour; dip in egg mixture, and dredge in breadcrumbs, shaking off excess.

2. Cook chicken in hot oil in a large ovenproof skillet over medium-high heat 3 to 4 minutes on each side or until golden. Top chicken with ham and cheese.

3. Bake chicken in skillet at 350° for 8 minutes or until cheese is melted. Serve over Garlic-Herb Pasta; top with Sautéed Grape Tomatoes.

GARLIC-HERB PASTA

½   cup butter, softened

1   garlic clove, pressed

⅔   cup chopped fresh basil

¼   cup chopped fresh parsley

¼   tsp. table salt

8   oz. cooked vermicelli

1. Stir together first 5 ingredients in a small bowl. Toss cooked pasta with ¼ cup garlic butter.

SAUTÉED GRAPE TOMATOES

1   pt. grape tomatoes, halved

1   Tbsp. light brown sugar

3   Tbsp. balsamic vinegar

¼   tsp. table salt

1   tsp. olive oil

2   Tbsp. thinly sliced fresh basil

1. Sauté tomatoes and next 3 ingredients in hot oil in a small skillet over medium-high heat 2 to 3 minutes. Remove from heat, and stir in basil.

PECAN CHICKEN AND TORTELLINI

WITH HERBED BUTTER SAUCE

makes: 4 servings hands-on time: 30 min. total time: 30 min.

Look for chicken cutlets that are of even thickness to ensure even cooking.

2 **(9-oz.) packages refrigerated cheese-filled tortellini**

4 **(4-oz.) chicken breast cutlets**

½ **tsp. table salt**

¼ **tsp. freshly ground black pepper**

¾ **cup finely chopped pecans**

1 **large egg, lightly beaten**

3 **Tbsp. olive oil**

½ **cup butter**

3 **garlic cloves, thinly sliced**

3 **Tbsp. chopped fresh basil**

3 **Tbsp. chopped fresh parsley**

¼ **cup (1 oz.) shredded Parmesan cheese**

1. Prepare tortellini according to package directions.

2. Meanwhile, sprinkle chicken with salt and pepper. Place pecans in a shallow bowl. Place egg in a second bowl. Dip chicken in egg mixture, allowing excess to drip off. Dredge chicken in pecans, pressing firmly for pecans to adhere.

3. Cook chicken in hot oil in a large nonstick skillet over medium-high heat 2 minutes on each side or until done. Remove from skillet; wipe skillet clean.

4. Melt butter in skillet over medium heat. Add garlic, and sauté 5 to 7 minutes or until garlic is caramel colored and butter begins to turn golden brown. Immediately remove from heat, and stir in basil, parsley, and tortellini. Sprinkle with cheese. Serve immediately with chicken.

SPRINGTIME PASTA WITH BACON

makes: 6 to 8 servings   hands-on time: 15 min.   total time: 30 min.

Enjoy this colorful dish warm or chilled; leftovers are perfect for a brown bag lunch the next day. Add grilled shrimp kabobs and a crisp Sauvignon Blanc for a relaxing meal with friends.

1   (16-oz.) package orec-chiette pasta

1   cup frozen sweet peas

1½ cups fresh snow peas

8   radishes, cut into wedges

2   large carrots, grated

2   green onions, thinly sliced

⅓   cup coarsely chopped fresh parsley

¼   cup lemon juice

¼   cup olive oil

6   thick bacon slices, cooked and crumbled

4   oz. crumbled goat cheese (optional)

1. Cook pasta according to package directions, adding sweet peas and snow peas during last minute of cooking time. Drain.

2. Toss pasta mixture with radishes and next 5 ingredients; add table salt and freshly ground black pepper to taste. Sprinkle with bacon and, if desired, crumbled goat cheese.

Pasta Pointer

1 (16-oz.) package farfalle (bow-tie) pasta may be substituted.

GRILLED FILLETS

WITH PECANS AND GREEN BEAN RAVIOLI

makes: 4 servings   hands-on time: 16 min.   total time: 30 min.

The ravioli and green beans cook together so cleanup is fast.

- **4   (4-oz.) beef tenderloin fillets**
- **1   tsp. table salt**
- **½   tsp. freshly ground black pepper**
- **1   (20-oz.) package refrigerated cheese-filled ravioli**
- **1   (8-oz.) package fresh small green beans**
- **½   cup butter**
- **3   garlic cloves, thinly sliced**
- **½   cup chopped toasted pecans**
- **1   Tbsp. chopped fresh sage**
- **½   cup (2 oz.) shredded Parmesan cheese**

1. Preheat grill to 350° to 400° (medium-high) heat. Sprinkle fillets with salt and pepper. Grill, covered with grill lid, 5 to 8 minutes on each side or until a meat thermometer inserted into thickest portion registers 145°. Let stand 10 minutes.

2. Meanwhile, cook ravioli and green beans in boiling water to cover in a Dutch oven 4 to 5 minutes or until green beans are crisp-tender. Drain.

3. Melt butter in skillet over medium heat. Add garlic, and sauté 5 to 7 minutes or until garlic is caramel colored and butter begins to brown. Remove from heat, and stir in pecans, sage, and hot pasta mixture. Sprinkle with cheese. Serve immediately with fillets.

ROQUEFORT NOODLES

makes: 6 to 8 servings hands-on time: 20 min. total time: 20 min.

Don't skimp on the quality of the cheese in this recipe. Roquefort offers unequaled flavor.

1 **(12-oz.) package wide egg noodles**

1 **Tbsp. jarred chicken soup base**

½ **tsp. olive oil**

½ **cup butter**

6 **to 8 green onions, sliced**

4 **to 6 oz. Roquefort cheese, crumbled**

1 **(8-oz.) container sour cream**

Serve this "stroganoff" type dish with steak tips.

PASTA POINTER

1. Prepare noodles according to package directions, adding chicken soup base and oil to water.

2. Meanwhile, melt butter in a large heavy skillet over medium heat. Add onions, and sauté 5 to 7 minutes or until tender. Reduce heat to medium-low, and stir in Roquefort cheese, stirring constantly, until cheese is melted. Remove from heat, and stir in sour cream until blended and smooth.

3. Toss together Roquefort cheese sauce and hot cooked egg noodles. Add seasoned pepper to taste.

Note: We tested with Superior Touch® Better Than Bouillon® Chicken Base.

SHRIMP DESTIN LINGUINE

makes: 2 to 3 servings   hands-on time: 30 min.   total time: 30 min.

For a little kick, add a pinch of dried crushed red pepper just before serving.

1½ lb. unpeeled, large raw shrimp

1   (9-oz.) package refrigerated linguine

¼   cup butter

¼   cup olive oil

¼   cup chopped green onions

2   garlic cloves, minced

1   Tbsp. dry white wine

2   tsp. fresh lemon juice

½   tsp. table salt

¼   tsp. coarsely ground black pepper

1   Tbsp. chopped fresh dill

1   Tbsp. chopped fresh parsley

If fresh shrimp is unavailable, thaw frozen uncooked shrimp.

1. Peel shrimp, leaving tails on, if desired. Devein, if desired.

2. Prepare pasta according to package directions.

3. Meanwhile, melt butter with oil in a large skillet over medium-high heat; add green onions and garlic, and sauté 4 to 5 minutes or until onions are tender. Add shrimp, wine, and next 3 ingredients. Cook over medium heat, stirring occasionally, 3 to 5 minutes or just until shrimp turn pink. Stir in dill and parsley. Remove shrimp with a slotted spoon, reserving sauce in skillet.

4. Add hot cooked pasta to sauce in skillet, tossing to coat. Transfer pasta to a serving bowl, and top with shrimp.

VIRGINIA HAM PASTA

makes: 6 to 8 servings hands-on time: 30 min. total time: 30 min.

If the cream sauce becomes too thick, loosen it with some reserve pasta hot water.

- 2 (8.8-oz.) packages fettuccine pasta
- ¼ lb. country ham, cut into ⅛-inch-thick strips (about ¾ cup)
- 2 Tbsp. olive oil
- 3 shallots, thinly sliced
- 8 oz. assorted wild mushrooms, sliced (optional)
- 1 garlic clove, thinly sliced
- 1 cup Viognier or dry white wine
- ½ cup frozen sweet peas (optional)
- ⅓ cup coarsely chopped fresh flat-leaf parsley
- ¼ cup heavy cream
- 3 Tbsp. butter
- ¼ tsp. freshly ground black pepper
- 1 cup freshly grated Pecorino Romano cheese

1. Prepare pasta according to package directions.

2. Meanwhile, sauté ham in hot oil in a large skillet over medium heat 2 minutes or until lightly browned and crisp. Add shallots; sauté 1 minute. Add mushrooms, if desired, and garlic, and cook, stirring often, 2 minutes or until mushrooms are tender. Stir in wine, and cook 5 minutes or until reduced by half.

3. Add peas, if desired, next 4 ingredients, and ½ cup cheese, stirring until cheese begins to melt and cream begins to thicken. Stir in hot cooked pasta, and toss until coated. Serve immediately with remaining ½ cup cheese.

CHIPOTLE-BACON MAC AND CHEESE

makes: 10 servings   hands-on time: 40 min.   total time: 1 hour, 20 min.

Smoky and rich best describe this new school mac and cheese. For a twist, try cavatappi pasta. Its twists and turns deliciously trap the creamy sauce.

- 3   tsp. sea salt, divided
- 1   (16-oz.) package cavatappi pasta
- 2   Tbsp. corn oil, divided
- ½   cup butter
- 1   small onion, diced
- 3   Tbsp. all-purpose flour
- 3   cups half-and-half
- 2   cups heavy cream
- 1   tsp. ground white pepper
- 3   cups freshly grated smoked Cheddar cheese
- 1   cup freshly grated Cheddar cheese
- 1   tsp. ground chipotle chile pepper
- 6   cooked bacon slices, chopped
- ¾   cup panko (Japanese breadcrumbs)

1. Preheat oven to 350°. Bring 1 gal. water and 1½ tsp. sea salt to a boil in a Dutch oven; add pasta. Cook 8 to 9 minutes or until al dente; drain. Toss with 1 Tbsp. oil.

2. Melt butter in a large saucepan over medium-high heat. Add onion, and sauté 4 to 5 minutes or until tender. Add flour, and cook, whisking constantly, 1 to 2 minutes or until smooth. (Do not brown flour.) Add half-and-half, next 2 ingredients, and remaining 1½ tsp. sea salt, and bring to a simmer. Cook, whisking constantly, 5 to 6 minutes or until thickened. Gradually add cheeses, stirring until blended. Transfer mixture to a large bowl; stir in cooked pasta. Spoon into a lightly greased 13- x 9-inch baking dish.

3. Sauté chipotle pepper in remaining 1 Tbsp. hot corn oil in a small skillet over medium heat 30 seconds or until mixture begins to smoke. Remove from heat, and quickly stir in bacon and panko until coated. Sprinkle mixture over pasta.

4. Bake at 350° for 15 to 20 minutes or until golden and crisp on top. Serve immediately.

GUSSIED UP MAC 'N' CHEESE

makes: 10 to 12 servings   hands-on time: 35 min.   total time: 1 hour

Andouille sausage ups the flavor factor and makes this an easy-to-serve one-dish meal. Add a salad on the side for a complete meal.

1   **(16-oz.) package cavatappi pasta**

½   **lb. andouille sausage, casings removed**

4   **cups heavy cream**

1   **(16-oz.) package processed cheese (such as Velveeta), cut into 1-inch cubes**

2   **cups (8 oz.) freshly shredded smoked Cheddar cheese**

½   **cup freshly shredded aged Gouda cheese**

½   **cup freshly shredded Parmigiano-Reggiano cheese**

1   **(5-oz.) package unsalted kettle-cooked potato chips, crumbled***

1. Preheat oven to 375°. Prepare pasta according to package directions for al dente.

2. Meanwhile, cut sausage lengthwise into quarters. Cut each quarter into ¼-inch-thick pieces.

3. Sauté sausage in a Dutch oven over medium-high heat 3 minutes or until browned around edges; drain on paper towels.

4. Bring cream to a simmer in Dutch oven over medium-high heat; reduce heat to low, and stir in cheese product. Cook, stirring constantly, until cheese is melted. Stir in sausage and remaining cheeses; cook, stirring constantly, until cheeses are melted. Remove from heat; stir in hot cooked pasta.

5. Pour mixture into a buttered 3-qt. baking dish or 12 (8-oz.) ramekins; top with potato chips. Bake at 375° for 20 minutes or until bubbly and browned. Remove from oven, and let stand 5 minutes.

* Lightly salted potato chips may be substituted.

Little Helpers

Have your little ones stand at the counter to learn how to shred cheese. Teach them how the box holes shred cheese differently.

FOUR-CHEESE MACARONI

makes: 8 servings hands-on time: 40 min. total time: 1 hour, 15 min.

If the breadcrumb topping browns too quickly, cover the baking dish with non-stick aluminum foil.

12 oz. cavatappi pasta

½ cup butter

½ cup all-purpose flour

½ tsp. ground red pepper

3 cups milk

2 cups (8 oz.) freshly shredded white Cheddar cheese

1 cup (4 oz.) freshly shredded Monterey Jack cheese

1 cup (4 oz.) freshly shredded fontina cheese

1 cup (4 oz.) freshly shredded Asiago cheese

1½ cups soft, fresh breadcrumbs

½ cup chopped cooked bacon

½ cup chopped pecans

2 Tbsp. butter, melted

1. Preheat oven to 350°. Prepare pasta according to package directions.

2. Meanwhile, melt ½ cup butter in a Dutch oven over low heat; whisk in flour and ground red pepper until smooth. Cook, whisking constantly, 1 minute. Gradually whisk in milk; cook over medium heat, whisking constantly, 6 to 7 minutes or until milk mixture is thickened and bubbly. Remove from heat.

3. Toss together Cheddar cheese and next 3 ingredients in a medium bowl; reserve 1½ cups cheese mixture. Add remaining cheese mixture and hot cooked pasta to sauce, tossing to coat. Spoon into a lightly greased 13- x 9-inch baking dish. Top with reserved 1½ cups cheese mixture.

4. Toss together breadcrumbs and next 3 ingredients; sprinkle over cheese mixture.

5. Bake at 350° for 35 to 40 minutes or until bubbly and golden brown.

PASTA-CHICKEN-BROCCOLI BAKE

makes: 6 to 8 servings hands-on time: 30 min. total time: 1 hour, 10 min.

Cheese-filled tortellini and a chopped pecan topping add extra flavor to kid-friendly Pasta-Chicken-Broccoli Bake, while broccoli and red bell pepper contribute pops of color throughout this one-dish meal.

½ cup butter

½ cup chopped sweet onion

½ cup chopped red bell pepper

2 garlic cloves, minced

¼ cup all-purpose flour

3 cups chicken broth

1½ cups half-and-half

½ cup dry white wine

1 cup (4 oz.) freshly shredded Parmesan cheese

¼ tsp. table salt

¼ tsp. ground red pepper

1 (20-oz.) package refrigerated cheese-and-spinach tortellini

4 cups chopped fresh broccoli

4 cups chopped cooked chicken

½ cup grated Parmesan cheese

15 round buttery crackers, crushed

½ cup chopped pecans

3 Tbsp. butter, melted

1. Preheat oven to 350°. Melt ½ cup butter in a Dutch oven over medium-high heat; add onion and next 2 ingredients, and sauté 5 to 6 minutes or until tender.

2. Add flour, stirring until smooth. Cook, stirring constantly, 1 minute. Whisk in broth, half-and-half, and white wine. Reduce heat to medium, and cook, stirring constantly, 6 to 8 minutes or until thickened and bubbly.

3. Remove from heat; add 1 cup cheese and next 2 ingredients, stirring until cheese melts. Stir in tortellini and next 2 ingredients. Spoon into a lightly greased 13- x 9-inch baking dish.

4. Stir together ½ cup grated cheese and next 3 ingredients. Sprinkle over casserole. Bake at 350° for 40 to 45 minutes or until bubbly.

CHICKEN DIVAN

makes: 6 to 8 servings   hands-on time: 30 min.   total time: 1 hour

Once described as "bride basic" and the meal to serve your mother-in-law, this classic is a hall-of-famer. No cream of mushroom soup, sour cream, or mayo in this from-scratch version.

12 oz. uncooked spaghetti

6 cups fresh broccoli florets

4 cups 1% low-fat milk

½ cup all-purpose flour

½ cup finely chopped shallots

1 tsp. olive oil

⅔ cup dry white wine

1 cup freshly grated Parmesan cheese

1 container from 1 (4.66-oz.) package concentrated chicken stock

1 tsp. table salt

1 tsp. freshly ground black pepper

4 cups shredded cooked chicken

1 cup (4 oz.) shredded white Cheddar cheese

1. Preheat oven to 375°. Cook pasta according to package directions, adding broccoli during last 2 to 3 minutes of cooking time.

2. Meanwhile, gradually whisk milk into flour in a bowl until smooth. Sauté shallots in hot oil in a Dutch oven over medium-high heat 1 to 2 minutes or until tender. Add wine, and cook 3 to 4 minutes or until reduced by half. Add milk mixture, and cook, whisking constantly, 7 to 8 minutes or until thickened and bubbly. Whisk in Parmesan cheese and next 3 ingredients until blended.

3. Drain pasta mixture well. Remove shallot mixture from heat, and stir in chicken and hot cooked pasta mixture. Spoon into a lightly greased 13- x 9-inch baking dish; sprinkle with Cheddar cheese. Place dish on an aluminum foil-lined baking sheet.

4. Bake at 375° for 30 to 35 minutes or until golden brown and bubbly.

Shred a rotisserie chicken instead of cooking chicken separately.

SPEED IT UP!

NEW TUNA CASSEROLE

makes: 8 servings hands-on time: 35 min. total time: 1 hour, 15 min.

Our take on the classic hits the high notes: creamy, cheesy, fresh, and crunchy. Resist digging into the casserole right out of the oven. Letting it stand for 10 minutes allows it to firm up to the perfect consistency.

- 1 **(16-oz.) package ziti pasta**
- 1 **(8-oz.) package haricots verts (thin green beans), cut into 1-inch pieces**
- 6 **Tbsp. butter, divided**
- 2 **medium leeks, thinly sliced**
- 2 **(4-oz.) packages fresh gourmet mushroom blend**
- ¼ **cup all-purpose flour**
- 3 **cups heavy cream**
- 1 **cup organic vegetable broth**
- 2 **cups (8 oz.) shredded sharp white Cheddar cheese**
- 6 **Tbsp. grated Parmesan cheese, divided**
- ¾ **tsp. kosher salt**
- ½ **tsp. freshly ground black pepper**
- 1 **(12-oz.) can solid white tuna in spring water, drained**
- 2 **Tbsp. chopped fresh chives**
- 1 **Tbsp. chopped fresh tarragon or parsley**
- ¼ **cup crushed potato chips**
- ¼ **cup panko (Japanese breadcrumbs)**
- 2 **Tbsp. butter, melted**

Garnish: sliced fresh chives

1. Preheat oven to 350°. Prepare pasta according to package directions.

2. Meanwhile, cook green beans in boiling salted water to cover 30 seconds to 1 minute or until crisp-tender; drain. Plunge into ice water to stop the cooking process; drain.

3. Melt 2 Tbsp. butter in a large skillet over medium-high heat. Add leeks, and sauté 2 minutes; add mushrooms, and sauté 5 minutes or until lightly browned. Transfer leek mixture to a small bowl. Wipe skillet clean.

4. Melt 4 Tbsp. butter in skillet over medium heat; whisk in flour, and cook, whisking constantly, 2 minutes. Gradually whisk in cream and broth. Bring mixture to a boil, stirring often. Reduce heat to medium-low; gradually whisk in Cheddar cheese and 4 Tbsp. Parmesan cheese until smooth. Stir in salt and pepper.

5. Stir cream mixture into pasta. Stir in tuna, next 2 ingredients, beans, and leek mixture; transfer to a lightly greased 13- x 9-inch baking dish.

6. Stir together potato chips, next 2 ingredients, and remaining 2 Tbsp. Parmesan cheese in a small bowl; sprinkle over pasta mixture.

7. Bake at 350° for 35 to 40 minutes or until bubbly. Let stand 10 minutes before serving.

BEEF STROGANOFF

makes: 6 to 8 servings   hands-on time: 15 min.   total time: 3 hours, 15 min.

Browning the sirloin tips before going into the slow cooker boosts the richness in flavor.

¼   cup all-purpose flour

2   lb. beef sirloin tips

½   tsp. table salt

½   tsp. freshly ground black pepper

2   Tbsp. olive oil

2   medium onions, chopped

2   (8-oz.) packages sliced fresh mushrooms

1½   cups beef broth

2   Tbsp. tomato paste

1   Tbsp. Dijon mustard

1½   cups sour cream

¼   cup dry sherry (optional)

Hot cooked egg noodles

Chopped fresh parsley (optional)

Pasta Pointer

Using beef sirloin tips saves time, but you can also purchase top sirloin and cut it into thin slices.

1. Place flour in a shallow dish. Sprinkle beef with salt and pepper; dredge in flour. Heat a large skillet over medium-high heat; add oil. Add beef; cook 7 minutes or until browned, stirring occasionally, reserving drippings in skillet. Transfer to a greased 5-qt. slow cooker. Add onion and mushrooms to drippings in skillet; cook, stirring often, 3 minutes or until tender.

2. Meanwhile, combine broth, tomato paste, and mustard. Add broth mixture to skillet, stirring to loosen particles from bottom of skillet. Pour over beef in slow cooker.

3. Cover and cook on LOW 3 hours or until beef is tender. Just before serving, stir in sour cream and, if desired, sherry. Serve over noodles. Sprinkle with parsley, if desired.

CAJUN CHICKEN PASTA

makes: 4 servings hands-on time: 35 min. total time: 35 min.

One easy way to kick up the flavor in a dish is to add Cajun seasoning. Here, the seasoning is sprinkled on the chicken strips before they're sautéed and tossed into the linguine-vegetable mixture.

12 oz. uncooked linguine

2 lb. chicken breast strips

1 Tbsp. Cajun seasoning

1¼ tsp. table salt, divided

¼ cup butter

1 small red bell pepper, thinly sliced*

1 small green bell pepper, thinly sliced*

1 (8-oz.) package fresh mushrooms

2 green onions (white and light green parts only), sliced*

1½ cups half-and-half

¼ tsp. lemon pepper

¼ tsp. dried basil

¼ tsp. garlic powder

Garnish: chopped green onions

1. Prepare pasta according to package directions.

2. Meanwhile, sprinkle chicken evenly with Cajun seasoning and 1 tsp. salt. Melt ¼ cup butter in a large nonstick skillet over medium-high heat; add chicken, and sauté 5 to 6 minutes or until done. Remove chicken.

3. Add bell peppers, mushrooms, and green onions to skillet, and sauté 9 to 10 minutes or until vegetables are tender and liquid evaporates.

4. Return chicken to skillet; stir in half-and-half, next 3 ingredients, and remaining ¼ tsp. salt. Cook, stirring often, over medium-low heat 3 to 4 minutes or until thoroughly heated. Add linguine; toss to coat. Serve immediately.

* ½ (16-oz.) bag frozen sliced green, red, and yellow bell peppers and onion may be substituted.

THREE-CHEESE BAKED PASTA

makes: 8 to 10 servings hands-on time: 10 min. total time: 40 min.

Prepare up to one day ahead; cover and refrigerate. Let stand at room temperature 30 minutes, and bake as directed. Ziti pasta is shaped in long, thin tubes; penne or rigatoni pasta may be substituted.

1   (16-oz.) package ziti pasta

2   (10-oz.) containers Alfredo sauce

1   (8-oz.) container sour cream

1   (15-oz.) container ricotta cheese

2   large eggs, lightly beaten

¼   cup grated Parmesan cheese

¼   cup chopped fresh parsley

1½ cups (6 oz.) mozzarella cheese

1. Preheat oven to 350°. Cook ziti according to package directions; drain and return to pot.

2. Stir together Alfredo sauce and sour cream; toss with ziti until evenly coated. Spoon half of ziti mixture into a lightly greased 13- x 9-inch baking dish.

3. Stir together ricotta cheese and next 3 ingredients; spread evenly over pasta mixture. Spoon remaining pasta mixture evenly over ricotta cheese layer; sprinkle with mozzarella cheese.

4. Bake at 350° for 30 minutes or until bubbly.

CLASSIC CHICKEN TETRAZZINI

makes: 8 to 10 servings hands-on time: 20 min. total time: 55 min.

To simplify and speed up dinner, use rotisserie chicken in this Italian dish. Although sizes vary, a whole chicken yields about 3 to 3½ cups, so you'll need two chickens. Reserve any leftover chicken for another use.

1½ **(8-oz.) packages vermicelli**

½ **cup butter**

½ **cup all-purpose flour**

4 **cups milk**

½ **cup dry white wine**

2 **Tbsp. chicken bouillon granules**

1 **tsp. seasoned pepper**

2 **cups freshly grated Parmesan cheese, divided**

4 **cups diced cooked chicken**

1 **(6-oz.) jar sliced mushrooms, drained**

¾ **cup slivered almonds**

1. Preheat oven to 350°. Prepare pasta according to package directions.

2. Meanwhile, melt butter in a Dutch oven over low heat; whisk in flour until smooth. Cook 1 minute, whisking constantly. Gradually whisk in milk and wine; cook over medium heat, whisking constantly, 8 to 10 minutes or until mixture is thickened and bubbly. Whisk in bouillon granules, seasoned pepper, and 1 cup Parmesan cheese.

3. Remove from heat; stir in diced cooked chicken, sliced mushrooms, and hot cooked pasta.

4. Spoon mixture into a lightly greased 13- x 9-inch baking dish; sprinkle with slivered almonds and remaining 1 cup Parmesan cheese.

5. Bake at 350° for 35 minutes or until bubbly.

An Italian classic, Chicken Tetrazzini can be made ahead. Freeze an unbaked casserole up to one month, if desired. Thaw overnight in refrigerator. Let stand 30 minutes at room temperature, and bake as directed.

SPEED IT UP!

SWEDISH MEATBALLS

makes: 6 servings hands-on time: 14 min. total time: 3 hours, 14 min.

A recipe that's versatile and uses convenience foods—what could be easier? Shop the freezer section to find already-prepared meatballs for this slow-cooker dish. The meatballs can be served over noodles for a main dish or as a hot appetizer.

1	**(32-oz.) package frozen fully cooked meatballs**
2	**Tbsp. vegetable oil**
¼	**cup all-purpose flour**
½	**tsp. table salt**
¼	**tsp. garlic powder**
¼	**tsp. freshly ground black pepper**
⅛	**tsp. ground nutmeg**

2	**cups chicken broth**
½	**cup white wine**
½	**cup sour cream**
2	**Tbsp. chopped fresh parsley**
½	**cup red currant jelly (optional)**

Hot cooked noodles

Garnish: chopped fresh parsley

1. Cook meatballs in a large skillet over medium-high heat 5 minutes, turning occasionally until browned on all sides.

2. Place meatballs in a 4-qt. slow cooker, reserving drippings in skillet. Reduce heat to low; add oil to skillet. Whisk in flour and next 4 ingredients until smooth. Increase heat to medium; cook, whisking constantly, 1 minute. Gradually whisk in chicken broth and wine. Cook, whisking frequently, 4 minutes or until slightly thickened. Pour gravy over meatballs. Cover and cook on LOW 3 hours.

3. Remove meatballs from slow cooker with a slotted spoon, and place in a serving bowl. Add sour cream, parsley, and, if desired, jelly to gravy, whisking until blended. Pour over meatballs. Serve over hot cooked noodles.

CHEESY HAM AND NOODLES

makes: 6 servings   hands-on time: 9 min.   total time: 3 hours, 9 min.

Rich, creamy, and ready-to-use Alfredo sauce forms the foundation for this slow-cooker casserole. Convenience never tasted so good.

12 oz. uncooked linguine

3   cups half-and-half

2   cups (8 oz.) shredded Swiss cheese

1   cup frozen sweet peas

1   Tbsp. Dijon mustard

1   (12-oz.) lean ham steak, chopped

1   (10-oz.) container refrigerated Alfredo sauce

1. Bring water to a boil in a 4-qt. saucepan. Cook linguine 5 minutes; drain. Transfer pasta to a lightly greased 4-qt. slow cooker. Add half-and-half, 1 cup cheese, and next 4 ingredients, stirring gently to blend. Sprinkle with remaining 1 cup cheese. Cover and cook on LOW 3 hours or until pasta is tender.

Pasta Pointer

This family-friendly pasta dish is adaptable. Use your favorite type of frozen peas, and substitute whipping cream and Gruyère cheese for easy alternatives to the half-and-half and Swiss cheese.

CINCINNATI 5-WAY CHILI

makes: 4 servings   hands-on time: 13 min.   total time: 6 hours, 13 min.

The unusual name comes from the five ways this dish is served: plain; over spaghetti; over spaghetti topped with grated cheese; over spaghetti topped with cheese and onions; and over spaghetti topped with cheese, onions, and beans.

1½   lb. ground sirloin
1   large onion, chopped
2   garlic cloves, minced
2   Tbsp. chili powder
1½   Tbsp. unsweetened cocoa
1   Tbsp. apple cider vinegar
1   Tbsp. Worcestershire sauce
1   tsp. ground allspice
1   tsp. ground cinnamon
½   tsp. table salt

¼   tsp. ground red pepper
1   bay leaf
1   (12-oz.) bottle German beer
1   (6-oz.) can tomato paste

Hot cooked spaghetti

Shredded sharp Cheddar cheese

Diced onion

1   (15-oz.) can kidney beans, drained and rinsed

1. Cook beef, onion, and garlic in a large nonstick skillet coated with cooking spray over medium-high heat 8 minutes or until browned. Stir in chili powder, next 10 ingredients, and ½ cup water. Transfer chili mixture to a 4- to 5-qt. slow cooker. Cover and cook on LOW 6 hours. Discard bay leaf.

2. Serve chili over hot cooked pasta. Top with cheese, diced onion, and kidney beans.

QUICK CHICKEN PICCATA

makes: 4 servings hands-on time: 30 min. total time: 30 min.

Lemon juice adds an acidic punch to this classic dish. Be sure to serve it with extra lemon wedges.

1   lb. skinned and boned chicken breasts

½   tsp. table salt

½   tsp. black pepper

½   cup Italian-seasoned breadcrumbs

2   Tbsp. olive oil

¼   cup chicken broth

3   Tbsp. fresh lemon juice

2   Tbsp. butter

2   Tbsp. chopped fresh parsley

1   (12-oz.) package angel hair pasta, cooked

Garnish: lemon wedges

1. Cut each chicken breast in half horizontally. Place between 2 sheets of heavy-duty plastic wrap; flatten to ¼-inch thickness, using a rolling pin or the flat side of a meat mallet.

2. Sprinkle chicken evenly with salt and pepper; lightly dredge in bread-crumbs.

3. Cook half of chicken in 1 Tbsp. hot oil in a large nonstick skillet over medium-high heat 2 minutes on each side or until golden brown and done. Remove chicken to a serving platter, and cover with aluminum foil. Repeat procedure with remaining chicken and 1 Tbsp. olive oil.

4. Add broth and lemon juice to skillet, and cook, stirring to loosen browned bits from bottom of skillet, until sauce is slightly thickened. Remove from heat; add butter and parsley, stirring until butter melts. Pour sauce over chicken, and serve over warm noodles.

ONE-DISH CHICKEN PASTA

makes: 6 servings hands-on time: 30 min. total time: 30 min.

Bake 2 or 3 large chicken breasts to yield 3 cups of chopped chicken.

- 1 (12-oz.) package farfalle (bow-tie) pasta
- 5 Tbsp. butter, divided
- 1 medium onion, chopped
- 1 medium-size red bell pepper, chopped
- 1 (8-oz.) package fresh mushrooms, quartered
- ⅓ cup all-purpose flour
- 3 cups chicken broth
- 2 cups milk
- 3 cups chopped cooked chicken
- 1 cup (4 oz.) shredded Parmesan cheese
- 1 tsp. freshly ground black pepper
- ½ tsp. table salt

Toppings: toasted sliced almonds, chopped fresh flat-leaf parsley, shredded Parmesan cheese

1. Prepare pasta according to package directions. Meanwhile, melt 2 Tbsp. butter in a Dutch oven over medium heat. Add onion and bell pepper; sauté 5 minutes or until tender. Add mushrooms; sauté 4 minutes. Remove from Dutch oven.

2. Melt remaining 3 Tbsp. butter in Dutch oven over low heat; whisk in flour until smooth. Cook, whisking constantly, 1 minute. Gradually whisk in chicken broth and milk; cook over medium heat, whisking constantly, 5 to 7 minutes or until thickened and bubbly.

3. Stir chicken, sautéed vegetables, and hot cooked pasta into sauce. Add cheese, pepper, and salt. Serve with desired toppings.

CHICKEN SPAGHETTI

makes: 8 servings hands-on time: 30 min. total time: 2 hours, 10 min.

Feel free to purchase chicken pieces but note the cooking time will be shorter.

- 1 (3-lb.) whole chicken
- 2 large Spanish onions, chopped
- 1 cup chopped celery
- 1 cup chopped green onions
- 1 medium-size green bell pepper, chopped
- 3 garlic cloves, chopped
- 2 Tbsp. bacon drippings
- 1 (15-oz.) can tomato sauce
- 1 (10¾-oz.) can tomato soup
- ⅓ cup tomato paste
- 2 Tbsp. Worcestershire sauce
- 1 tsp. hot sauce
- 1 bay leaf
- ¾ cup chopped fresh flat-leaf parsley
- 1 (16-oz.) package spaghetti, cooked

Garnishes: fresh parsley leaves, Parmesan cheese

1. If applicable, remove giblets from chicken, and reserve for another use.

2. Sauté Spanish onions and next 4 ingredients in hot drippings in a large Dutch oven over medium-high heat 8 to 10 minutes or until tender. Stir in tomato sauce, next 5 ingredients, 1 cup water, and chicken. Bring to a boil; reduce heat to medium-low, and simmer 1 hour or until chicken is done. Remove chicken, reserving tomato mixture in Dutch oven. Cool chicken 20 minutes.

3. Meanwhile, simmer reserved tomato mixture, stirring occasionally, 20 minutes.

4. Skin, bone, and shred chicken; stir into tomato mixture. Stir in parsley. Add table salt and freshly ground pepper to taste. Discard bay leaf. Serve over spaghetti.

PASTA POINTER

Make this yummy dish a little healthier by substituting whole grain spaghetti.

ZUCCHINI-MINT PASTA

makes: 4 to 6 main-dish or 6 to 8 side-dish servings hands-on time: 18 min. total time: 18 min.

- 2 **Tbsp. butter**
- 2 **Tbsp. olive oil**
- 2 **shallots, diced**
- 1½ **lb. small zucchini, sliced**
- 1 **garlic clove, minced**
- 2 **tsp. loosely packed lemon zest**
- 2 **Tbsp. fresh lemon juice**
- 1 **tsp. kosher salt**
- ½ **tsp. freshly ground black pepper**

- 1 **(9-oz.) package refrigerated fettuccine pasta, cooked, or 1 (8.8-oz.) package pappardelle pasta, cooked**
- ½ **cup thinly sliced fresh mint**
- ½ **cup chopped toasted walnuts**
- ¼ **cup freshly grated Parmesan cheese**
- 1 **cup (4 oz.) crumbled feta cheese**

1. Melt butter with olive oil in a large nonstick skillet over medium-high heat; add shallots, and sauté 2 minutes. Add zucchini; sauté 5 minutes or until zucchini is tender. Stir in minced garlic, and cook 1 minute.

2. Remove from heat; stir in lemon zest, lemon juice, kosher salt, and freshly ground black pepper. Toss in cooked pasta, fresh mint, walnuts, and Parmesan cheese.

3. Sprinkle with feta cheese just before serving.

Pasta Pointer

Add cooked shrimp for a heartier main, or white beans for a vegetarian option.

LEMONY BROCCOLI RABE PASTA

makes: 4 to 6 servings   hands-on time: 20 min.   total time: 30 min.

Reinvent pasta night with this easy family favorite. Goat cheese accompanies Parmesan in this 30-minute dish made with your choice of filei, penne, or fusilli pasta.

2	tsp. kosher salt
1	lb. broccoli rabe, trimmed and cut into 3-inch pieces
1	(16- to 17-oz.) package filei, penne, or fusilli
3	Tbsp. butter
1	Tbsp. olive oil
2	garlic cloves, chopped
¾	tsp. dried crushed red pepper
2	tsp. loosely packed lemon zest
¼	cup freshly grated Parmesan cheese
1	Tbsp. lemon juice
1	(4-oz.) package goat cheese, crumbled

1. Bring 4 qt. water to a boil in a large Dutch oven. Add 2 tsp. kosher salt, return to a boil, and stir in broccoli rabe. Cook 1 minute or until crisp-tender; drain. Plunge into ice water to stop the cooking process; drain.

2. Cook pasta in Dutch oven according to package directions; drain, reserving ½ cup hot pasta water.

3. Melt butter with oil in Dutch oven over medium heat; add garlic, and sauté 1 to 2 minutes or until tender. Add red pepper and lemon zest; cook, stirring constantly, 1 minute. Stir in broccoli rabe; cook, stirring constantly, 1 minute. Stir in hot cooked pasta, reserved pasta water, Parmesan cheese, and lemon juice; cook 1 to 2 minutes. Add kosher salt and black pepper to taste. Top with cheese.

PASTA POINTER

Before you drain your perfectly cooked pasta (al dente, of course!), scoop out at least 1 cup of that rich, starchy pasta water to make an easy pan sauce. We often use ¼ to ½ cup in some pasta dishes, but for most recipes save a little extra in case you want a looser sauce.

EASY SKILLET PIMIENTO MAC AND CHEESE

makes: 2 to 4 servings hands-on time: 15 min. total time: 15 min.

In the South, pimiento cheese might as well be its own food group. It's a crowd-pleaser as an appetizer and sandwich spread. Now it plays a starring role in mac and cheese.

- ½ (16-oz.) package penne pasta
- 2 Tbsp. all-purpose flour
- 1½ cups milk
- 1 cup (4 oz.) shredded sharp Cheddar cheese
- 1 (4-oz.) jar diced pimiento, drained
- ¾ tsp. table salt
- ¼ tsp. freshly ground black pepper
- Pinch of paprika

1. Prepare pasta according to package directions.

2. Meanwhile, whisk together flour and ¼ cup milk. Add flour mixture to remaining milk, whisking until smooth.

3. Bring milk mixture to a boil in a large skillet over medium heat; reduce heat to medium-low, and simmer, whisking constantly, 3 to 5 minutes or until smooth. Stir in cheese and next 4 ingredients until smooth. Stir in pasta, and cook 1 minute or until thoroughly heated. Serve immediately.

Easy Skillet Green Chile Mac and Cheese: Substitute 1 cup (4 oz.) shredded Monterey Jack cheese for Cheddar cheese and 1 (4-oz.) can chopped green chiles, undrained, for diced pimiento. Proceed with recipe as directed.

Easy Skillet Whole Grain Mac and Cheese: Substitute ½ (13.5-oz.) package whole grain penne pasta for regular. Proceed with recipe as directed.

Pasta Pointer

This recipe is easily doubled to feed a crowd. Top it with buttered breadcrumbs for some crunch.

Classic Italian Pastas

Break out your
red-checkered tablecloth
for these Italian favorites.

MEATBALL PASTA BAKE

makes: 8 to 10 servings   hands-on time: 30 min.   total time: 1 hour, 10 min.

Orange juice and fennel give this quick supper bright, fresh flavor. Chop fennel as you would an onion, or omit it, if desired.

- 1 (16-oz.) package penne pasta
- 1 small sweet onion, chopped
- 1 medium fennel bulb, thinly sliced (optional)
- 2 Tbsp. olive oil
- 3 garlic cloves, minced
- 1 tsp. fennel seeds
- 2 (24-oz.) jars marinara sauce
- 2 (14-oz.) packages frozen beef meatballs, thawed
- 1 cup fresh orange juice
- ¾ cup organic chicken broth
- 1 tsp. firmly packed orange zest
- 1 medium-size red bell pepper, chopped
- ½ tsp. kosher salt
- 1 cup torn fresh basil
- 1½ (8-oz.) packages fresh mozzarella cheese slices

Garnish: fresh basil leaves

1. Preheat oven to 350°. Prepare pasta according to package directions.

2. Meanwhile, sauté onion and fennel bulb in hot oil in a Dutch oven over medium heat 8 to 10 minutes or until tender. Add garlic and fennel seeds, and sauté 1 minute. Stir in marinara sauce and next 6 ingredients; increase heat to medium-high, and bring to a boil. Reduce heat to medium-low; cover and simmer 10 minutes. Remove from heat, and stir in basil, cooked pasta, and table salt to taste. Transfer to a lightly greased 13- x 9-inch baking dish. Place dish on an aluminum foil-lined baking sheet. Top with cheese.

3. Bake at 350° for 25 minutes or until bubbly.

BAKED ZITI WITH SAUSAGE

makes: 8 servings hands-on time: 30 min. total time: 55 min.

San Marzano tomatoes are known for their sweet flavor. Consider trying them in place of regular crushed tomatoes in the sauce.

12   oz. uncooked ziti pasta

4   oz. pancetta or bacon, diced

1   large onion, chopped

3   garlic cloves, chopped

1   (1-lb.) package ground Italian sausage

1   cup dry red wine

1   (28-oz.) can crushed tomatoes

½   cup firmly packed torn fresh basil

½   tsp. kosher salt

½   tsp. dried crushed red pepper

1   cup ricotta cheese

1   (8-oz.) package shredded mozzarella cheese, divided

½   cup grated Parmesan cheese

Garnish: chopped fresh parsley

1. Preheat oven to 350°. Prepare ziti according to package directions for al dente.

2. Meanwhile, cook pancetta in a large skillet over medium-high heat 3 minutes. Add onion and garlic, and sauté 3 minutes or until onion is tender. Add sausage, and cook, stirring constantly, 5 minutes or until meat crumbles and is no longer pink. Add wine, and cook 3 minutes. Stir in tomatoes and next 3 ingredients. Reduce heat to low, and cook, stirring occasionally, 3 minutes.

3. Stir ricotta and 1 cup mozzarella cheese into hot cooked pasta. Lightly grease a 13- x 9-inch baking dish with cooking spray. Transfer pasta mixture to prepared dish, and top with sausage mixture. Sprinkle with Parmesan cheese and remaining 1 cup mozzarella cheese.

4. Bake at 350° for 25 to 30 minutes or until bubbly.

BURST TOMATO AND HERB SPAGHETTI

makes: 4 servings hands-on time: 30 min. total time: 40 min.

Cover the skillet to prevent splatters as the tomatoes burst.

2   medium zucchini, chopped

2   Tbsp. olive oil, divided

3   garlic cloves, sliced

¼   tsp. dried crushed red pepper

1   tsp. kosher salt, divided

3   pt. grape tomatoes

½   tsp. freshly ground black pepper

1   (8-oz.) package spaghetti

1   cup coarsely chopped fresh basil

¼   cup coarsely chopped fresh flat-leaf parsley

Shaved Parmesan cheese

Let the kids watch the tomatoes burst. They'll love it!

LITTLE HELPERS

1. Sauté zucchini in 1 Tbsp. hot oil in a large skillet over medium-high heat 5 minutes or until zucchini begins to brown. Add garlic, red pepper, and ¼ tsp. kosher salt; cook, stirring often, 4 to 5 minutes or until garlic begins to brown. Remove from skillet.

2. Add tomatoes, black pepper, and remaining 1 Tbsp. oil and ¾ tsp. kosher salt to skillet; cook, stirring occasionally, 2 minutes. Cover, reduce heat to medium, and cook, stirring occasionally, 10 minutes or until tomatoes begin to burst.

3. Cook pasta according to package directions; drain, reserving ¼ cup hot pasta water. Add pasta, reserved hot pasta water, and zucchini mixture to skillet along with basil and parsley; toss. Top with cheese.

ZUCCHINI-AND-SPINACH LASAGNA

makes: 4 servings hands-on time: 15 min. total time: 55 min.

Looking for an alternative to meaty, cheesy lasagna? Try this colorful, veggie-rich version. It's a delicious way to go vegetarian for supper.

- 1 **(8-oz.) container whipped chive-and-onion cream cheese**
- 1 **(15-oz.) container ricotta cheese**
- ⅓ **cup chopped fresh basil**
- 1 **tsp. table salt**
- 5 **medium zucchini, thinly sliced (about 2½ lb.)**
- 2 **Tbsp. olive oil**
- 1 **(10-oz.) package fresh spinach**
- 2 **garlic cloves, pressed**
- 6 **no-boil lasagna noodles**
- 1 **(7-oz.) package shredded mozzarella cheese**

Garnish: fresh basil leaves

1. Preheat oven to 425°. Stir together first 4 ingredients in a bowl.

2. Sauté zucchini in hot oil in a large skillet over medium-high heat 3 to 4 minutes or until lightly browned. Add spinach; gently toss until wilted. Add garlic; cook 1 minute.

3. Spoon one-third of vegetables into a lightly greased 9-inch square baking dish; top with 2 noodles and one-third of ricotta mixture. Repeat twice. Sprinkle with mozzarella.

4. Bake, covered with lightly greased aluminum foil, at 425° for 25 to 30 minutes or until bubbly and noodles are tender. Uncover and bake 5 to 10 more minutes or until golden. Let stand 10 minutes.

FRESH TOMATO-AND-ASPARAGUS GNOCCHI

makes: 4 servings hands-on time: 25 min. total time: 30 min.

Use asparagus with thicker, sturdier stems rather than the pencil-thin variety for this dish. Peak season for this popular vegetable is February through June.

- 1 lb. fresh asparagus
- 1 (16-oz.) package gnocchi
- ½ cup chopped sweet onion
- 2 Tbsp. olive oil
- 4 garlic cloves, pressed
- 4 large tomatoes, seeded and chopped
- ½ cup chopped fresh basil
- 1 tsp. table salt
- ½ tsp. freshly ground black pepper
- Grated Parmesan cheese

1. Cut asparagus into 2-inch pieces, discarding tough ends. Fill a 3-qt. saucepan three-fourths full with salted water. Bring to a boil; add asparagus and gnocchi, and cook 2 to 4 minutes or until tender. Drain.

2. Sauté onion in hot oil in a medium skillet over medium-high heat 5 to 6 minutes or until tender; add garlic, and cook 1 minute. Add tomatoes, and cook 3 to 5 minutes. Stir in basil, salt, pepper, and asparagus mixture. Sprinkle each serving with Parmesan cheese; serve immediately.

Pasta Pointer

Look for gnocchi in the refrigerator section near the other fresh pastas and on the pasta aisle.

CHICKEN PARMIGIANA

makes: 4 servings   hands-on time: 20 min.   total time: 50 min.

Skip the green can of grated Parmesan cheese and grate your own for the best flavor and melting consistency.

- **4   skinned and boned chicken breasts (1 lb.)**
- **½   tsp. table salt**
- **¼   tsp. freshly ground black pepper**
- **2   large egg whites**
- **¾   cup crushed cornflakes cereal**
- **½   cup freshly grated Parmesan cheese**
- **1   tsp. dried Italian seasoning**
- **½   cup all-purpose flour**
- **Vegetable cooking spray**
- **Pasta sauce**
- **Shredded mozzarella cheese**
- **Hot cooked spaghetti**

1. Preheat oven to 425°. Sprinkle chicken with salt and pepper. Whisk egg whites just until foamy.

2. Place a lightly greased wire rack in a 15- x 10-inch jelly-roll pan. Stir together cornflakes, Parmesan cheese, and Italian seasoning.

3. Dredge chicken in flour, shaking off excess. Dip chicken in egg white, and dredge in cornflake mixture. Lightly coat chicken on each side with cooking spray; arrange chicken on wire rack.

4. Bake at 425° for 25 to 30 minutes or until golden brown and done.

5. Top each chicken breast with your favorite pasta sauce and shredded mozzarella. Bake 5 more minutes or until cheese is melted. Serve over hot cooked spaghetti.

FETTUCCINE WITH ZUCCHINI AND PECANS

makes: 6 servings   hands-on time: 25 min.   total time: 25 min.

A cheesy, buttery sauce coats ribbons of fettuccine studded with fresh zucchini.

- **1** **(12-oz.) package fettuccine**
- **2** **Tbsp. butter**
- **2** **Tbsp. olive oil**
- **1** **lb. small zucchini, shredded**
- **2** **garlic cloves, minced**
- **¾** **cup coarsely chopped toasted pecans**
- **1** **cup freshly grated Asiago cheese**
- **¼** **cup thinly sliced fresh basil**

1. Prepare fettuccine according to package directions.

2. Meanwhile, melt butter with olive oil in a large nonstick skillet over medium-high heat; add zucchini and garlic, and sauté 3 to 4 minutes or until zucchini is tender. Toss with hot cooked fettuccine, pecans, Asiago cheese, and basil. Add table salt and freshly ground black pepper to taste. Serve immediately.

Use the shredder attachment on a food processor for even faster prep of zucchini.

SPEED IT UP!

SWEET POTATO GNOCCHI
WITH MUSHROOMS

makes: 8 servings hands-on time: 25 min. total time: 25 min.

These pillowy Italian dumplings take on new flavor with a hint of sweetness that balances deliciously with "meaty" portobello mushrooms. The gnocchi make an excellent accompaniment with your favorite meat or poultry dish, or can also stand alone as a lunch or simple supper dish.

1   **(16-oz.) package sweet potato gnocchi**

6   **Tbsp. butter, divided**

1   **(8-oz.) package sliced baby portobello mushrooms**

4   **garlic cloves, thinly sliced**

3   **Tbsp. sliced fresh shallots**

2   **Tbsp. chopped fresh flat-leaf parsley**

1   **Tbsp. thinly sliced fresh sage**

1   **tsp. kosher salt**

¼   **tsp. freshly ground black pepper**

Toppings: freshly shaved Parmesan cheese, freshly ground black pepper, chopped fresh parsley

1. Prepare gnocchi according to package directions. Keep warm.

2. Meanwhile, melt 2 Tbsp. butter in a large skillet over medium-high heat. Add mushrooms; sauté 3 to 5 minutes or until lightly browned. Add garlic and shallots; sauté 2 minutes or until tender. Remove from skillet. Wipe skillet clean.

3. Melt remaining 4 Tbsp. butter in skillet over medium-high heat; cook 2 to 3 minutes or until lightly browned. Stir in parsley, sage, and mushroom mixture. Add hot cooked gnocchi, and toss gently. Stir in salt and pepper. Serve immediately with desired toppings.

BUTTERNUT SQUASH RAVIOLI WITH MUSHROOMS

makes: 8 servings hands-on time: 25 min. total time: 25 min.

Thanks to store-bought ravioli, this easy weeknight dinner comes together quickly. Offer this indulgent ravioli as a side dish or as a meatless main dish.

- 2 **(8-oz.) packages refrigerated butternut squash-filled ravioli**
- 6 **Tbsp. butter, divided**
- 1 **(8-oz.) package sliced baby portobello mushrooms**
- 4 **garlic cloves, thinly sliced**
- 3 **Tbsp. sliced shallots**
- 2 **Tbsp. chopped fresh flat-leaf parsley**
- 1 **Tbsp. thinly sliced fresh sage**
- 1 **tsp. kosher salt**
- ¼ **tsp. freshly ground black pepper**

Toppings: freshly shaved Parmesan cheese, freshly ground black pepper, chopped fresh parsley

1. Prepare ravioli according to package directions. Keep warm.

2. Melt 2 Tbsp. butter in a large skillet over medium-high heat. Add mushrooms; sauté 3 to 5 minutes or until lightly browned. Add garlic and shallots; sauté 2 minutes or until tender. Remove from skillet. Wipe skillet clean.

3. Melt remaining 4 Tbsp. butter in skillet over medium-high heat; cook 2 to 3 minutes or until lightly browned. Stir in parsley, sage, and mushroom mixture. Add hot cooked ravioli, and toss gently. Stir in salt and pepper. Serve immediately with desired toppings.

Cheese Ravioli with Mushrooms: Substitute 2 (8-oz.) packages refrigerated three-cheese-filled ravioli for butternut squash ravioli.

Sweet Potato Gnocchi with Mushrooms: Substitute 1 (16-oz.) package sweet potato gnocchi for ravioli.

ROASTED VEGETABLE GNOCCHI WITH SPINACH-HERB PESTO

makes: 4 servings   hands-on time: 10 min.   total time: 45 min.

If yellow squash isn't available, substitute other seasonal vegetables.

- 6 yellow squash (about 1¼ lb.)
- 8 sweet mini bell peppers
- 2 Tbsp. olive oil
- 1 tsp. table salt
- ½ tsp. coarsely ground black pepper
- 1 (16-oz.) package gnocchi*
- Spinach-Herb Pesto
- ½ (6-oz.) package fresh baby spinach
- ¼ to ⅓ cup (1 to 1½ oz.) freshly shredded Parmesan cheese

1. Preheat oven to 425°. Cut squash into 1-inch pieces. Cut bell peppers in half lengthwise; remove seeds. Stir together squash, bell peppers, oil, salt, and ground pepper. Arrange vegetables in a single layer on a jelly-roll pan, and bake at 425° for 15 minutes. Stir and bake 5 more minutes or until tender and golden.

2. Meanwhile, cook gnocchi according to package directions in a Dutch oven; drain. Return to Dutch oven. Add Spinach-Herb Pesto to gnocchi, and toss to coat. Add squash mixture and spinach, and gently toss to combine. Sprinkle with Parmesan cheese. Serve immediately.

* Medium-size pasta shells may be substituted.

SPINACH-HERB PESTO

makes: ¾ cup
hands-on time: 15 min.
total time: 15 min.

- ½ (6-oz.) package fresh baby spinach
- 1 Tbsp. chopped fresh cilantro
- 1 Tbsp. chopped fresh basil
- 1 tsp. loosely packed lemon zest
- 2 Tbsp. lemon juice
- 1 tsp. chopped fresh mint
- 1 garlic clove, minced
- ¼ tsp. table salt
- ½ cup (2 oz.) freshly shredded Parmesan cheese
- ¼ cup olive oil

1. Pulse first 8 ingredients in a food processor 6 or 7 times or until finely chopped. Add Parmesan cheese and oil; process until smooth, stopping to scrape down sides as needed. Use immediately, or store in refrigerator up to 48 hours. If chilled, let stand at room temperature 30 minutes before using; stir until blended.

FETTUCCINE-AND-ASPARAGUS AL BURRO

makes: 3 to 4 servings hands-on time: 30 min. total time: 30 min.

Al burro means "buttered." This simple sauce is a more authentic version of today's popular Alfredo, which calls for whipping cream. Buy a high-quality cheese—it makes a difference.

1   lb. fresh thin asparagus

4   to 6 oz. thick pancetta slices, diced

1   (9-oz.) package refrigerated fettuccine

2   Tbsp. butter

3   Tbsp. extra virgin olive oil

½   cup freshly shredded Parmigiano-Reggiano cheese

2   Tbsp. chopped fresh flat-leaf parsley

¼   tsp. table salt

¼   tsp. freshly ground black pepper

Toppings: shaved Parmesan cheese, freshly ground black pepper

1. Cut asparagus into 1½-inch pieces, discarding tough ends.

2. Sauté pancetta in a large skillet over medium heat 5 minutes or until crisp; remove from skillet.

3. Cook fettuccine and asparagus in boiling salted water to cover 2 to 3 minutes. Drain, reserving ¼ cup pasta water.

4. Melt butter with oil in skillet over medium heat; add hot cooked pasta and asparagus, cheese, and next 3 ingredients. Toss to coat, adding enough reserved pasta water to make a glossy sauce. Remove from heat; sprinkle with pancetta. Serve immediately with desired toppings.

FAST-AND-FRESH SAUSAGE RAGU

makes: 6 to 8 servings   hands-on time: 20 min.   total time: 40 min.

Use your favorite breakfast or Italian sausage. For a finer texture, break up the sausage as it cooks using a potato masher.

- **1** **(16-oz.) package riga-toni pasta**
- **1** **(1-lb.) package ground pork sausage with sage**
- **1** **medium onion, diced**
- **1** **medium zucchini, diced**
- **2** **medium carrots, diced**
- **3** **garlic cloves, pressed**
- **¼** **tsp. dried crushed red pepper**
- **1** **(6-oz.) can tomato paste**
- **1** **cup dry red wine**
- **1** **(28-oz.) can diced tomatoes with basil, garlic, and oregano**

Freshly grated Parmesan cheese

1. Cook pasta according to package directions; drain, reserving ½ cup pasta water.

2. Meanwhile, cook sausage in a large 2-inch-deep skillet over medium-high heat, stirring often, 5 minutes or until sausage crumbles and is no longer pink. Add onion, zucchini, and carrots; cook, stirring often, 8 to 10 minutes or until tender. Add garlic and red pepper, and cook, stirring often, 1 to 2 minutes or until garlic is tender. Add tomato paste, and cook, stirring constantly, 1 to 2 minutes. Add wine and reserved pasta water; cook 2 minutes, stirring to loosen bits from bottom of skillet.

3. Add tomatoes, and bring to a boil. Reduce heat to medium, and simmer, stirring occasionally, 10 minutes. Add table salt and black pepper to taste. Spoon sausage mixture over pasta; sprinkle with cheese.

Look for gluten-free rigatoni pasta as an alternative.

Pasta Pointer

SPINACH-AND-HERB PASTATTA

makes: 8 servings   hands-on time: 40 min.   total time: 1 hour, 45 min.

Introducing the pastatta: a comforting, hearty casserole that's a cross between baked pasta and frittata.

- 1   **(10-oz.) package frozen chopped spinach, thawed**
- 1   **(16-oz.) package mezze penne pasta**
- 2½   **Tbsp. butter**
- 3   **large shallots, sliced**
- 2   **Tbsp. all-purpose flour**
- 1½   **cups half-and-half**
- ½   **cup ricotta cheese**
- 1   **cup (4 oz.) freshly shredded Asiago cheese, divided**
- 10   **large eggs, lightly beaten**
- ⅓   **cup loosely packed fresh flat-leaf parsley, coarsely chopped**
- 1   **Tbsp. finely chopped chives**
- 2   **tsp. kosher salt**
- 1   **tsp. freshly ground black pepper**

Garnishes: fresh flat-leaf parsley leaves, freshly shredded Parmesan cheese

1. Preheat oven to 325°. Drain spinach well, pressing between paper towels.

2. Prepare pasta according to package directions.

3. Meanwhile, melt butter in a medium saucepan over medium heat; add shallots, and sauté 5 minutes or until golden brown. Whisk in flour until smooth; cook 1 minute, whisking constantly. Gradually whisk in half-and-half; cook over medium heat, whisking constantly, until thickened and bubbly. Whisk in ricotta and ½ cup Asiago cheese until smooth. Remove from heat.

4. Whisk eggs in a bowl until frothy. Fold in shallot mixture, spinach, parsley, and next 3 ingredients. Stir in cooked pasta.

5. Sprinkle ¼ cup Asiago cheese on inside rim of a lightly greased 9-inch springform pan. Pour pasta mixture into pan.

6. Bake at 325° for 55 minutes to 1 hour and 10 minutes or until set. Let stand 10 minutes. Remove sides of pan. Sprinkle with remaining ¼ cup Asiago cheese.

TOMATO-BASIL LASAGNA ROLLS

makes: 10 servings hands-on time: 35 min. total time: 1 hour, 25 min.

Canned artichokes give the rich filling its meaty heft. Feel free to sub sautéed mushrooms or spinach.

10 uncooked lasagna noodles

1 cup finely chopped sweet onion

2 tsp. olive oil

3 garlic cloves, minced and divided

1 (24-oz.) jar tomato-and-basil pasta sauce

1½ tsp. sugar

¼ tsp. dried crushed red pepper

1 cup low-fat ricotta cheese

2 oz. ⅓-less-fat cream cheese, softened

1 (14-oz.) can baby artichoke hearts, drained and quartered

1 large egg white, lightly beaten

¼ cup torn fresh basil

¼ cup (1 oz.) freshly shredded Parmesan cheese

Toppings: fresh basil, freshly shredded Parmesan cheese

1. Preheat oven to 350°. Cook pasta according to package directions for al dente. Arrange in a single layer on a piece of lightly greased aluminum foil or wax paper.

2. Sauté onion in hot oil in a 3-qt. saucepan over medium heat 7 to 8 minutes or until caramelized. Add two-thirds of minced garlic, and cook, stirring constantly, 1 minute. Stir in tomato sauce and next 2 ingredients. Bring mixture to a boil, stirring often. Reduce heat to low; simmer, stirring often, 5 minutes. Remove from heat.

3. Stir together ricotta and cream cheese until smooth. Stir in artichoke hearts, next 3 ingredients, and remaining minced garlic. Spread ¼ cup cheese mixture on 1 noodle. Roll up firmly, and place, seam side down, into a lightly greased 11- x 7-inch baking dish. Repeat with remaining noodles and cheese mixture. Spoon tomato sauce over lasagna rolls.

4. Bake, covered, at 350° for 45 to 50 minutes or until thoroughly heated and bubbly. Let stand 5 minutes. Sprinkle with desired toppings.

PIZZA CASSEROLE DELUXE

makes: 10 servings   hands-on time: 40 min.   total time: 1 hour, 15 min.

Win over all of the kids and grown-ups in your house with this new instant classic that feeds a crowd. The combination of fresh and packaged mozzarella gives it great flavor and lots of melted cheesiness.

1 (1-lb.) package ground mild Italian sausage

2 garlic cloves, minced

1 Tbsp. olive oil

1 (26-oz.) jar marinara sauce

1 tsp. kosher salt, divided

½ medium-size red onion, chopped

½ medium-size red bell pepper, chopped

½ medium-size green bell pepper, chopped

½ (8-oz.) package sliced baby portobello mushrooms

1 cup sliced black olives

½ cup pepperoni slices, chopped

1 (16-oz.) package rigatoni pasta

3 Tbsp. butter

3 Tbsp. all-purpose flour

3 cups half-and-half

8 oz. fresh mozzarella, shredded (2 cups)

½ cup grated Parmesan cheese

½ tsp. freshly ground black pepper

1 (8-oz.) package shredded mozzarella cheese

8 to 10 pepperoni slices

1. Preheat oven to 350°. Cook sausage and garlic in hot oil over medium-high heat, stirring often, until sausage crumbles and is no longer pink. Remove with a slotted spoon, reserving drippings in skillet. Drain sausage mixture on paper towels, and transfer to a medium bowl. Stir marinara sauce and ½ tsp. salt into sausage mixture.

2. Sauté onion and next 3 ingredients in hot drippings 5 minutes or until tender; stir in olives and chopped pepperoni. Reserve ¼ cup onion mixture.

3. Prepare pasta according to package directions in a large Dutch oven.

4. Meanwhile, melt butter in a heavy saucepan over low heat; whisk in flour until smooth. Cook, whisking constantly, 1 minute. Gradually whisk in half-and-half; cook over medium heat, whisking constantly, 7 to 10 minutes or until mixture is thickened and bubbly. Stir in fresh mozzarella cheese, Parmesan cheese, pepper, and remaining ½ tsp. salt. Pour sauce over pasta in Dutch oven, stirring to coat. Stir in onion mixture.

5. Transfer pasta mixture to a lightly greased 13- x 9-inch baking dish, and top with sausage mixture, packaged mozzarella cheese, reserved ¼ cup onion mixture, and pepperoni slices.

6. Bake at 350° for 30 minutes or until cheese is melted and lightly browned. Let stand 5 minutes before serving.

ONE-POT PASTA
WITH TOMATO-BASIL SAUCE

makes: 6 servings hands-on time: 20 min. total time: 50 min.

This dish is a revelation. Throw all of your ingredients into one pot over medium-high heat, and about 25 minutes later you'll have noodles perfectly coated in a luscious tomato-basil sauce.

- 12 oz. casarecce or fusilli pasta
- 1 (28-oz.) can diced tomatoes
- 2 cups chicken broth
- ½ medium-size yellow onion, sliced
- 4 garlic cloves, sliced
- 1 tsp. dried oregano
- ⅓ cup firmly packed fresh basil leaves
- 2 tsp. kosher salt
- 1 Tbsp. olive oil
- ¼ tsp. dried crushed red pepper (optional)
- 1 (6-oz.) package fresh baby spinach
- Freshly ground black pepper
- Freshly grated Parmesan cheese

1. Place first 9 ingredients and, if desired, dried crushed red pepper in a Dutch oven in order of ingredient list. Cover and bring to a boil over medium-high heat (about 12 to 15 minutes). Reduce heat to medium-low, and cook, covered, 10 to 12 minutes or until pasta is slightly al dente, stirring at 5-minute intervals.

2. Remove from heat, and stir in spinach. Cover and let stand 10 minutes. Stir just before serving. Sprinkle with black pepper. Serve with Parmesan cheese.

Pasta Pointer

For a seafood variation, prepare recipe as directed, stirring in 1 lb. peeled large, raw shrimp, deveined, with spinach in Step 2.

FRESH VEGETABLE LASAGNA

makes: 8 servings hands-on time: 30 min. total time: 1 hour, 35 min.

For easier slicing, don't cut the 10 minutes resting time short. It's necessary for the lasagna to hold together.

- 4 medium zucchini, halved lengthwise and thinly sliced (about 1½ lb.)
- 1 (8-oz.) package sliced fresh mushrooms
- 2 garlic cloves, minced
- 1 medium-size red bell pepper, chopped
- 1 medium-size yellow bell pepper, chopped
- 1 yellow onion, chopped
- ½ tsp. table salt
- 1½ cups fat-free ricotta cheese
- 1 large egg
- 2 cups (8 oz.) shredded part-skim mozzarella cheese, divided
- ½ cup freshly grated Parmesan cheese, divided
- 5 cups marinara sauce
- 1 (8-oz.) package no-boil lasagna noodles

Garnish: fresh basil leaves

1. Preheat oven to 450°. Bake zucchini, mushrooms, and garlic in a jelly-roll pan coated with cooking spray 12 to 14 minutes or until vegetables are crisp-tender, stirring halfway through. Repeat procedure with bell peppers and onion. Reduce oven temperature to 350°. Toss together vegetables and salt in a bowl.

2. Stir together ricotta, egg, 1½ cups shredded mozzarella cheese, and ¼ cup grated Parmesan cheese.

3. Spread 1 cup marinara sauce in a 13- x 9-inch baking dish coated with cooking spray. Top with 3 noodles, 1 cup sauce, one-third of ricotta mixture, and one-third of vegetable mixture; repeat layers twice, beginning with 3 noodles. Top with remaining noodles and 1 cup sauce. Sprinkle with remaining ½ cup shredded mozzarella and ¼ cup grated Parmesan.

4. Bake, covered, at 350° for 45 minutes. Uncover and bake 10 to 15 more minutes or until cheese is melted and golden. Let stand 10 minutes.

STUFFED ALFREDO CHICKEN

makes: 4 servings hands-on time: 25 min. total time: 1 hour, 25 min.

Three different cheeses plus spinach make this saucy dish a weeknight favorite. It's wonderful alongside egg noodles and crisp-tender green beans or asparagus.

4   skinned and boned chicken breasts

8   oz. ground mild Italian pork sausage

1   (1.25-oz.) envelope Alfredo sauce mix

1   cup (4 oz.) shredded mozzarella cheese

1   cup (4 oz.) shredded Parmesan cheese

1   (10-oz.) package frozen chopped spinach, thawed and drained

½   cup ricotta cheese

Hot cooked egg noodles

2   plum tomatoes, diced

1. Preheat oven to 350°. Place chicken between 2 sheets of heavy-duty plastic wrap, and flatten to ¼-inch thickness using a meat mallet or rolling pin. Set aside.

2. Cook sausage in a large skillet over medium-high heat, stirring often, 10 minutes or until sausage crumbles and is no longer pink; drain and set aside.

3. Prepare Alfredo sauce according to package directions; set aside.

4. Combine shredded mozzarella and Parmesan cheeses.

5. Stir together sausage, spinach, ricotta cheese, and ½ cup mozzarella cheese mixture. Spoon mixture evenly down center of each chicken breast, and roll up, jelly-roll fashion. Arrange chicken rolls, seam side down, in a lightly greased 2-qt. baking dish. Pour Alfredo sauce over chicken, and sprinkle evenly with remaining 1½ cups mozzarella cheese mixture.

6. Bake at 350° for 50 minutes to 1 hour or until chicken is done. Let stand 10 minutes. Cut chicken rolls into slices. Serve with sauce over hot cooked egg noodles; sprinkle evenly with diced tomatoes just before serving.

With supervision, let your kids pound the chicken.

LITTLE HELPERS

SPINACH-RAVIOLI LASAGNA

makes: 6 to 8 servings   hands-on time: 10 min.   total time: 45 min.

Although this dish calls for frozen ravioli, you can let the ravioli stand at room temperature for about 5 minutes before preparing the recipe to allow the frozen ravioli to separate more easily.

1   (6-oz.) package fresh baby spinach

⅓   cup refrigerated pesto sauce

1   (15-oz.) jar Alfredo sauce

¼   cup vegetable broth

1   (25-oz.) package frozen cheese-filled ravioli (do not thaw)

1   cup (4 oz.) shredded Italian six-cheese blend

1. Preheat oven to 375°. Chop spinach, and toss with pesto in a medium bowl.

2. Combine Alfredo sauce and vegetable broth. Spoon one-third of Alfredo sauce mixture (about ½ cup) into a lightly greased 2-qt. baking dish. Top with half of spinach mixture. Arrange half of ravioli in a single layer over spinach mixture. Repeat layers. Top with remaining Alfredo sauce.

3. Bake at 375° for 30 minutes. Remove from oven, and sprinkle with shredded cheese. Bake 5 minutes or until hot and bubbly.

Jarred Alfredo sauce and jarred pesto sauce make it much quicker to whip up this delicious weeknight dinner.

SPEED IT UP!

SAUCY MANICOTTI

makes: 7 servings hands-on time: 40 min. total time: 1 hour, 30 min.

With crusty cheese bubbling over and blanketing a thick meat sauce, this dish delivers a taste of Italy guaranteed to please everyone at your dinner table.

1   (8-oz.) package manicotti shells

1   (16-oz.) package Italian sausage, casings removed

1   large onion, chopped

9   garlic cloves, pressed

1   (26-oz.) jar seven-herb tomato pasta sauce

6   cups (24 oz.) shredded mozzarella cheese, divided

1   (15-oz.) container ricotta cheese

1   (8-oz.) container chive-and-onion cream cheese

¾   cup freshly grated Parmesan cheese

¾   tsp. freshly ground black pepper

1. Cook manicotti shells according to package directions for al dente.

2. Meanwhile, cook sausage, onion, and half of pressed garlic in a large Dutch oven over medium-high heat, stirring occasionally, 6 minutes or until sausage crumbles and is no longer pink. Stir in pasta sauce; bring to a boil. Remove from heat.

3. Preheat oven to 350°. Combine 4 cups mozzarella cheese, next 4 ingredients, and remaining pressed garlic in a large bowl, stirring until blended. Cut a slit down length of each cooked manicotti shell.

4. Spoon ¼ cup sauce into each of 7 lightly greased 8-oz. shallow baking dishes. Spoon cheese mixture into manicotti shells, gently pressing cut sides together. Arrange stuffed shells over sauce in dishes, seam sides down. Spoon remaining sauce (about ¾ cup per dish) over stuffed shells. Sprinkle with remaining 2 cups mozzarella cheese.

5. Bake, uncovered, at 350° for 50 minutes.

To bake in a single casserole dish, spoon 1 cup sauce into a lightly greased 13- x 9-inch baking dish. Arrange stuffed shells over sauce in dish. Top with remaining sauce and remaining mozzarella cheese. Bake, uncovered, at 350° for 50 minutes or until bubbly.

Pasta Pointer

PIZZA SPAGHETTI CASSEROLE

makes: 6 servings   hands-on time: 15 min.   total time: 55 min.

We preferred turkey pepperoni, so you don't get a greasy appearance. For a make-ahead dish, freeze the unbaked casserole up to one month. Thaw overnight in the refrigerator; let stand 30 minutes at room temperature, and bake as directed.

12	oz. uncooked spaghetti
½	tsp. table salt
1	(1-lb.) package mild ground pork sausage
2	oz. turkey pepperoni slices (about 30), cut in half
1	(26-oz.) jar tomato-and-basil pasta sauce
¼	cup grated Parmesan cheese
1	(8-oz.) package shredded Italian three-cheese blend

1. Preheat oven to 350°. Cook spaghetti with ½ tsp. salt according to package directions. Place in a lightly greased 13- x 9-inch baking dish.

2. Brown sausage in a large skillet over medium-high heat, stirring occasionally, 5 minutes or until meat crumbles and is no longer pink. Drain and set aside. Wipe skillet clean. Add pepperoni, and cook over medium-high heat, stirring occasionally, 4 minutes or until slightly crisp.

3. Top spaghetti in baking dish with sausage; pour pasta sauce over sausage. Arrange half of pepperoni slices evenly over pasta sauce. Sprinkle evenly with cheeses. Arrange remaining half of pepperoni slices evenly over cheese. Cover with non-stick or lightly greased aluminum foil.

4. Bake at 350° for 30 minutes; remove foil, and bake 10 more minutes or until cheese is melted and just begins to brown.

PAPPARDELLE BOLOGNESE

makes: 6 servings hands-on time: 15 min. total time: 6 hours, 15 min.

A staple of northern Italy's Bologna region, Bolognese is a thick, hearty meat sauce. Our version cooks to perfection in a slow cooker. Add a green salad and crusty bread and dinner's ready.

- 2 **Tbsp. olive oil**
- 2 **cups refrigerated pre-chopped celery, onion, and bell pepper mix**
- ½ **cup chopped carrot**
- 2 **garlic cloves, pressed**
- 1½ **lb. ground chuck**
- ¾ **tsp. table salt**
- ¾ **tsp. freshly ground black pepper**
- 2 **cups milk**
- 1½ **cups dry white wine**
- ¼ **tsp. freshly grated nutmeg**
- 1 **(28-oz.) can whole San Marzano tomatoes in tomato puree, undrained and chopped**

Hot cooked pappardelle pasta

Freshly grated Parmesan cheese

Chopped fresh parsley

1. Heat oil in a large nonstick skillet over medium-high heat. Add celery mixture and carrot; sauté 3 minutes or until tender. Add garlic; sauté 1 minute. Transfer vegetable mixture to a lightly greased 5-qt. slow cooker.

2. Add beef, salt, and pepper to pan; cook 5 minutes, stirring until beef crumbles and is no longer pink. Drain, if needed. Add beef mixture to vegetable mixture. Stir in milk and next 3 ingredients.

3. Cover and cook on HIGH 6 hours. Serve sauce over hot cooked pasta; if desired, sprinkle with Parmesan cheese and parsley.

Pasta Pointer

Pappardelle is pasta shaped like wide ribbons. If your store doesn't stock it, substitute the more narrow fettuccine or tagliatelle.

SHORTCUT RAVIOLI LASAGNA

makes: 4 to 6 servings hands-on time: 15 min. total time: 6 hours, 15 min.

A little planning goes a long way with this slow-cooker favorite. Keep these ingredients on hand because it's easy to assemble. Dinner's ready when you are!

1   **lb. ground round**

1   **cup refrigerated pre-chopped onion**

2   **garlic cloves, minced (optional)**

1   **(24-oz.) jar pasta sauce**

1   **(25-oz.) package frozen cheese-filled ravioli (do not thaw)**

1   **(8-oz.) package shredded Italian six-cheese blend**

1. Cook ground round, onion, and, if desired, minced garlic in a large skillet over medium-high heat, stirring occasionally, 8 minutes or until beef crumbles and is no longer pink. Drain, if needed.

2. Spoon ¾ cup pasta sauce into bottom of a lightly greased 4-qt. slow cooker. Layer half of ravioli, half of meat mixture, and 1 cup cheese over sauce. Repeat layers with ¾ cup sauce, remaining ravioli, and remaining meat mixture. Top with remaining sauce; sprinkle with remaining 1 cup cheese.

3. Cover and cook on LOW 6 hours or until pasta is tender.

PASTA POINTER

Use your favorite pasta sauce for this ultra-easy dish. We liked the flavor of Newman's Own.

BAKED FOUR-CHEESE SPAGHETTI WITH ITALIAN SAUSAGE

makes: 8 to 10 servings   hands-on time: 15 min.   total time: 3 hours, 25 min.

Cheese, please! Four types combine to produce an ooey-gooey merry mix of goodness. You can even start your dinner late in the day for this slow-cooker dish because it's ready in just over three hours.

- 8   oz. uncooked spaghetti
- 1   lb. Italian sausage (about 4 links), casings removed
- 1   (8-oz.) container refrigerated prechopped bell pepper-and-onion mix
- 2   tsp. jarred minced garlic
- 1   Tbsp. vegetable oil
- 1   (24-oz.) jar fire-roasted tomato and garlic pasta sauce
- 1   (16-oz.) package shredded sharp Cheddar cheese
- 1   (8-oz.) package shredded mozzarella cheese, divided
- 4   oz. fontina cheese, shredded
- ½   cup (2 oz.) preshredded Parmesan cheese

Garnish: thinly sliced fresh basil

1. Cook pasta according to package directions. Drain and return to pan.

2. Meanwhile, brown sausage, bell pepper mix, and garlic in oil in a large nonstick skillet over medium-high heat, stirring often, 8 to 10 minutes or until meat crumbles and is no longer pink. Drain. Stir meat mixture, pasta sauce, and Cheddar cheese into pasta. Spoon half of pasta mixture into a lightly greased 5-qt. slow cooker coated with cooking spray.

3. Combine mozzarella cheese and fontina cheese. Sprinkle half of mozzarella mixture over pasta mixture in slow cooker. Top with remaining pasta mixture, remaining mozzarella mixture, and Parmesan cheese. Cover and cook on LOW 3 hours. Let stand, covered, 10 minutes before serving.

PASTA POINTER

Open sausage casings using kitchen shears; then just squeeze the sausage into the pan for browning.

CHICKEN PARMESAN

makes: 6 servings hands-on time: 12 min. total time: 3 hours, 47 min.

With the countless ways to cook chicken in a slow cooker, this ranks among our favorites. The crispy Italian-seasoned panko coating helps keep the chicken moist and flavorful.

2	cups Italian-seasoned panko (Japanese breadcrumbs)
6	skinned and boned chicken breasts
2	large eggs, lightly beaten
4	Tbsp. olive oil, divided
1	(44-oz.) jar tomato-basil sauce
¾	tsp. table salt
½	tsp. freshly ground black pepper
1	(8-oz.) package shredded mozzarella cheese
¾	cup (3 oz.) shredded Parmesan cheese

Garnish: fresh oregano

1. Spread breadcrumbs on a large plate. Dip chicken in beaten egg, 1 breast at a time. Dredge chicken in breadcrumbs, pressing gently for crumbs to adhere.

2. Heat 2 Tbsp. oil in a large nonstick skillet over medium-high heat. Cook chicken, in 2 batches, 2 minutes on each side or until browned, adding remaining 2 Tbsp. oil with second batch.

3. Pour sauce into a lightly greased 6- or 7-qt. oval slow cooker. Arrange chicken in slow cooker over sauce. Sprinkle with salt and pepper. Cover and cook on HIGH 3½ hours. Add cheeses; cover and cook on HIGH 5 more minutes or until cheese melts.

WILD MUSHROOM PASTA ALFREDO
WITH WALNUTS

makes: 8 servings hands-on time: 6 min. total time: 2 hours, 6 min.

Try going vegetarian for a change. The hearty mushroom pasta gives this dish a "meaty" taste.

2   (15-oz.) jars Alfredo sauce

2   (9-oz.) packages refrigerated wild mushroom agnolotti pasta

1   cup (4 oz.) shredded Parmesan cheese

4   cups grape tomatoes

1   cup toasted walnut halves

Freshly ground black pepper

4   cups fresh baby spinach

Garnish: shredded Parmesan cheese

1. Spoon 1 cup Alfredo sauce into a lightly greased 3½- or 4-qt. slow cooker. Spread 1 package of pasta over sauce. Top with ½ cup cheese, 2 cups tomatoes, and ½ cup walnuts. Sprinkle with pepper to taste. Repeat layers. Top with 1 cup Alfredo sauce. Reserve remaining Alfredo sauce for other uses.

2. Cover and cook on HIGH 2 hours. Stir in spinach just before serving.

Pasta Pointer

Agnolotti are square ravioli packets typically filled with meat and/or vegetables.

SLOW-COOKER LASAGNA

makes: 6 servings   hands-on time: 15 min.   total time: 2 hours, 15 min.

Who knew you could make lasagna in a slow cooker? It comes together like classic lasagna in a dish, only it's layered in the slow cooker. For dash, we added Swiss chard.

1	**(28-oz.) can diced tomatoes, drained**
1	**(28-oz.) jar chunky pasta sauce**
3	**garlic cloves, finely chopped**
¼	**cup fresh oregano, chopped**
½	**tsp. kosher salt**
¾	**tsp. freshly ground black pepper, divided**
1	**(15-oz.) container ricotta cheese**

½	**cup fresh flat-leaf parsley, chopped**
½	**cup shredded Parmesan cheese**
1	**(12-oz.) package lasagna noodles**
1	**bunch Swiss chard, tough stems removed and torn into large pieces**
3	**cups (12 oz.) shredded mozzarella cheese**

1. In a medium bowl, combine tomatoes, sauce, garlic, oregano, salt, and ½ tsp. pepper. In another medium bowl, combine ricotta, parsley, Parmesan cheese, and remaining ¼ tsp. pepper. Spoon one-third of tomato mixture into a 6-qt. slow cooker.

2. Top with a single layer of noodles, breaking them to fit as necessary. Add half of Swiss chard. Dollop with one-third of ricotta mixture and one-third of remaining tomato mixture. Sprinkle with one-third of mozzarella cheese. Add another layer of noodles, and repeat with other ingredients. Finish with a layer of noodles and remaining ricotta mixture, tomato mixture, and mozzarella. Cover and cook on LOW for 2 to 3 hours or until noodles are tender.

If using a slow cooker smaller than a 6-qt. one, the cooking time may take an additional hour or more, and results may vary.

Pasta Pointer

SPAGHETTI AND MEATBALLS

makes: 6 to 8 servings hands-on time: 15 min. total time: 1 hour, 10 min.

Make traditional spaghetti and meatballs in a flash by taking a shortcut with frozen meatballs and an easy sauce of canned tomatoes, tomato pasta, and dried herbs.

1   (16-oz.) package spaghetti

2   (28-oz.) cans diced tomatoes

1   (6-oz.) can tomato paste

1   tsp. dried basil

1½ tsp. table salt

¼   tsp. freshly ground black pepper

⅛   tsp. dried oregano

⅛   tsp. ground red pepper

3   dozen frozen, cooked Italian-style meatballs, thawed

Garnishes: freshly grated Parmesan cheese, fresh oregano

1. Prepare spaghetti according to package directions.

2. Meanwhile, stir together tomatoes, next 6 ingredients, and 1 cup water in a large saucepan over medium-high heat. Reduce heat, and simmer, stirring occasionally, 40 minutes.

3. Add meatballs; simmer 20 minutes. Serve over pasta.

Let the kids help make this easy pasta sauce by having them stir occasionally.

LITTLE HELPERS

GLOBAL BOWLS

Travel around the world
with these flavorful dishes.

PORK PAD THAI

makes: 8 servings hands-on time: 30 min. total time: 41 min.

Pad Thai is a flavorful dish of stir-fried pork, carrots, bean sprouts, and green onions over a bed of rice noodles and coated with a spicy peanut butter sauce.

1½	lb. pork tenderloin, trimmed
2	Tbsp. canola oil
3	large eggs, lightly beaten
1	bunch green onions, cut into 2-inch pieces

Spicy Peanut Butter Sauce

1	(1-lb.) package rice noodles, cooked
2	cups matchstick carrots
2	cups bean sprouts
½	cup finely chopped dry-roasted peanuts

1. Cut pork into very thin pieces.

2. Stir-fry pork in hot oil in a large wok over medium heat 5 to 8 minutes or until done. Place pork in a bowl.

3. Add eggs to wok, and cook, stirring constantly, 1 minute or until set. Add pork and green onions to wok, and sauté 1 to 2 minutes. Stir in Spicy Peanut Butter Sauce and hot cooked noodles.

4. Divide pork mixture evenly between 8 plates. Place ¼ cup carrots onto left side of each plate and ¼ cup bean sprouts onto right side of each plate. Sprinkle each serving with 1 Tbsp. chopped peanuts. Serve immediately.

SPICY PEANUT BUTTER SAUCE

makes: about 2 cups
hands-on time: 10 min.
total time: 10 min.

½	cup creamy peanut butter
½	cup soy sauce
4	garlic cloves, chopped
¼	cup honey
2	Tbsp. rice wine vinegar
2	Tbsp. sesame oil
2	Tbsp. Asian Sriracha hot chili sauce
1	Tbsp. chopped fresh ginger
¼	tsp. ground red pepper
½	cup cold water

1. Process all ingredients in a food processor 10 to 12 seconds or until well blended.

BRISKET AND RICE NOODLES WITH PINEAPPLE SALSA

makes: 4 servings hands-on time: 15 min. total time: 25 min.

Pulled pork or cooked shrimp can stand in for the brisket.

1 Tbsp. kosher salt

½ (8.8-oz.) package thin rice noodles

½ fresh pineapple, peeled, cored, and finely chopped

1½ small Kirby cucumbers, seeded and sliced

⅓ cup thinly sliced red onion

2 Tbsp. chopped fresh cilantro

1½ Tbsp. seasoned rice wine vinegar

3 Tbsp. hoisin sauce

2 Tbsp. roasted peanut oil

2 Tbsp. fresh lime juice

1 Tbsp. fish sauce

1 tsp. Asian Sriracha hot chili sauce

4 cups shredded romaine lettuce

1 lb. shredded smoked beef brisket, warm

½ cup sliced pickled Peppadew peppers

½ cup assorted torn mint, basil, and cilantro

1. Microwave 8 cups water and 1 Tbsp. kosher salt at HIGH in a large microwave-safe glass bowl 2 minutes. Submerge noodles in water; let stand 20 minutes or until tender. Drain.

2. Meanwhile, toss together pineapple and next 4 ingredients; add table salt and black pepper to taste.

3. Whisk together hoisin sauce, next 4 ingredients, and 2 Tbsp. water. Combine drained noodles and 2 Tbsp. hoisin sauce mixture in a medium bowl, tossing to coat.

4. Divide lettuce among 4 bowls. Top with noodles, pineapple mixture, brisket, and peppers. Drizzle with desired amount of remaining hoisin mixture. Sprinkle with herbs, and serve immediately.

THAI-STYLE NOODLES

makes: 4 servings hands-on time: 15 min. total time: 15 min.

Look for Sriracha in the ethnic section of your local supermarket.

- 1 **(8-oz.) package wide lo-mein noodles**
- 2 **Tbsp. light brown sugar**
- 2 **tsp. loosely packed lime zest**
- 2 **Tbsp. fresh lime juice**
- 1½ **Tbsp. fish sauce**
- 1 **tsp. Asian Sriracha hot chili sauce**
- ½ **cup coarsely chopped roasted peanuts**
- ¼ **cup sliced green onions**
- ¼ **cup chopped fresh cilantro**

1. Prepare noodles according to package directions.

2. Meanwhile, whisk together brown sugar, lime zest, lime juice, fish sauce, and chili sauce in a large bowl. Stir in peanuts, green onions, and cilantro. Toss peanut sauce with lo-mein noodles. Serve immediately.

Substitute fettuccine if you can't find lo-mein noodles.

Pasta Pointer

SWEET-HOT ASIAN NOODLE BOWL

makes: 8 servings   hands-on time: 35 min.   total time: 50 min.

This Asian noodle bowl is great cold, so plan to take leftovers to work. Store your bottle of dark sesame oil in the fridge. The oil will solidify, so let it come to room temperature before measuring.

¾   cup rice wine vinegar

⅓   cup lite soy sauce

⅓   cup honey

2   Tbsp. minced fresh ginger

2   Tbsp. dark sesame oil

1   Tbsp. Asian Sriracha hot chili sauce

1   (16-oz.) package spaghetti

1   (15-oz.) can cut baby corn, drained and rinsed

1   (8-oz.) can sliced water chestnuts, drained and rinsed

1   large red bell pepper, thinly sliced

1   cup (about 4 oz.) thinly sliced snow peas

⅓   cup finely chopped green onions

¼   cup chopped fresh cilantro

1   Tbsp. toasted sesame seeds (optional)

1. Whisk together first 6 ingredients in a medium bowl; set aside.

2. Prepare spaghetti according to package directions; drain and return pasta to pot.

3. Pour vinegar mixture over hot cooked pasta. Add baby corn and next 5 ingredients, and toss to combine. Sprinkle with sesame seeds, if desired. Serve hot or cold.

FRIED NOODLES WITH SHRIMP

makes: 4 to 6 servings hands-on time: 30 min. total time: 30 min.

Sriracha, a hot sauce made from a fiery blend of chile peppers, garlic, vinegar, sugar, and salt, is a defining ingredient in Asian cooking.

- 1½ lb. unpeeled, large raw shrimp
- 1 (8-oz.) package Thai rice noodles
- 2 garlic cloves, minced
- ¼ cup vegetable oil
- 2 large eggs, lightly beaten
- 2 Tbsp. sugar
- 2 Tbsp. fish sauce
- 2 Tbsp. Asian Sriracha hot chili sauce
- 2 green onions, chopped
- 2 to 3 Tbsp. chopped peanuts
- ¼ cup chopped fresh cilantro
- Lime wedges (optional)

Thai rice noodles may be found in the Asian section of larger grocery stores or at Asian markets.

1. Peel shrimp; devein, if desired, and set aside.

2. Cook noodles in boiling water 3 to 4 minutes; drain.

3. Sauté garlic in hot vegetable oil in a large nonstick skillet over medium heat 2 minutes. Add shrimp, and cook 2 minutes or just until shrimp turn pink. Add beaten egg to shrimp mixture in skillet. Cook shrimp mixture over medium heat, without stirring, until egg begins to set. Stir until cooked, breaking up egg.

4. Add sugar, fish sauce, and chili sauce, stirring until blended. Add noodles, and cook 1 minute or until thoroughly heated. Sprinkle with onions, peanuts, and cilantro. Squeeze lime wedges over noodles, if desired.

SZECHUAN GINGER STIR-FRY WITH NOODLE PANCAKES

makes: 6 servings   hands-on time: 22 min.   total time: 30 min.

For assorted seafood, we used peeled, raw shrimp and fish fillets, cut into 1-inch pieces.

- ½ cup stir-fry sauce
- 1 garlic clove, pressed
- ½ tsp. cornstarch
- ½ tsp. dried crushed red pepper
- ¼ cup vegetable oil, divided
- 6 oz. fine egg noodles, cooked
- 1¼ lb. assorted seafood
- 1 Tbsp. minced fresh ginger
- ¼ to ½ tsp. hot chili oil
- 2 medium-size red or yellow bell peppers, cut into thin strips
- 1 (6-oz.) package frozen snow peas, thawed

Ramen noodles are a yummy substitution too.

Pasta Pointer

1. Stir together first 4 ingredients and ⅓ cup water; set aside.

2. Heat 2 Tbsp. vegetable oil in a 12-inch nonstick skillet or wok over medium-high heat. Add noodles, pressing evenly into bottom of skillet. Cook 8 minutes or until bottom is golden and crispy. Carefully invert onto a plate; return to skillet, crisp side up. Cook 5 minutes or until bottom is golden. Place on a serving platter, and cut into 6 wedges. Cover and keep warm.

3. Stir-fry seafood and ginger in 1 Tbsp. vegetable oil and chili oil in skillet 2 minutes; remove from skillet. Add remaining 1 Tbsp. vegetable oil, and stir-fry bell pepper and snow peas 2 minutes or until pepper is crisp-tender. Return seafood and stir-fry sauce mixture to skillet. Cook, stirring constantly, until mixture boils and thickens. Spoon over noodle wedges, and serve immediately.

CHICKEN SESAME NOODLES

makes: 6 servings   hands-on time: 23 min.   total time: 23 min.

This easy, breezy dinner calls for already-prepared grilled chicken strips. For a nutritional boost, be sure the multigrain pasta includes the word "whole" in the ingredients list as in "whole" wheat for maximum health benefits.

- **1   (14.5-oz.) package multigrain spaghetti**
- **½   cup Thai peanut sauce**
- **3   green onions, sliced**
- **½   cup diced red bell pepper**
- **2   Tbsp. chopped fresh cilantro (optional)**
- **1   Tbsp. fresh lime juice**
- **2   (6-oz.) packages fully cooked grilled chicken strips**
- **1   Tbsp. toasted sesame seeds**

1. Prepare spaghetti according to package directions. Toss with peanut sauce, green onions, red bell pepper, cilantro, if desired, and fresh lime juice. Stir in chicken. Sprinkle with toasted sesame seeds.

Shrimp Sesame Noodles: Prepare recipe as directed. Stir in 1 lb. peeled, medium-size cooked shrimp, deveined and cut in half lengthwise.

STICKY NOODLE BOWL

makes: 4 servings hands-on time: 15 min. total time: 30 min.

If you can't find steak strips, thinly slice flank steak.

1 **(11-oz.) box Asian-style noodles with soy-ginger sauce**

1 **(6-oz.) package fresh snow peas**

1 **small red bell pepper, thinly sliced**

½ **medium onion, thinly sliced**

2 **Tbsp. freshly grated ginger**

1 **Tbsp. olive oil**

1 **(8-oz.) package steak strips**

1 **tsp. minced garlic**

⅓ **cup vegetable broth**

1 **Tbsp. creamy peanut butter**

Toppings: chopped peanuts, chopped fresh cilantro, bean sprouts, lime wedges

1. Remove and reserve sauce and sesame seed topping packets from box of noodles. Cook noodles according to package directions, stirring in snow peas during last minute of cooking; drain.

2. Sauté bell pepper, onion, and ginger in hot oil in a large skillet over medium-high heat 3 minutes or until crisp-tender. Stir in strips and garlic; sauté 3 minutes or until thoroughly heated. Stir in cooked noodles, reserved sauce packet, vegetable broth, and peanut butter, tossing to coat. Cook, stirring constantly, 2 minutes or until peanut butter is melted and mixture is thoroughly heated.

3. Transfer noodle mixture to a large serving platter, and serve with desired toppings. Top with reserved sesame seed topping, if desired.

Shorten your time in the kitchen by accomplishing two things at once: While the pasta cooks, sauté the vegetables and steak strips.

Speed It Up!

SHRIMP SESAME NOODLES

makes: 4 servings hands-on time: 25 min. total time: 25 min.

Tahini is a smooth, thick paste made from ground sesame seeds. Popular in Middle Eastern cooking, tahini is a key ingredient in hummus.

¼	**cup lite soy sauce**
3	**Tbsp. tahini**
4	**tsp. rice vinegar**
2	**garlic cloves**
2	**tsp. sugar**
2	**tsp. grated fresh ginger**
¼	**tsp. ground red pepper**

2	**Tbsp. sesame oil**
2	**green onions, minced**
½	**lb. unpeeled, medium-size raw shrimp**
1	**Tbsp. vegetable oil**
1	**(5-oz.) package Japanese curly noodles, cooked**

1. Process first 7 ingredients and 2 Tbsp. water in a food processor until smooth, stopping to scrape down sides. With food processor running, pour sesame oil through food chute in a slow, steady stream; process until sauce is smooth. Stir in minced green onions.

2. Peel shrimp, and devein, if desired.

3. Heat vegetable oil in a large non-stick skillet or wok over medium-high heat 1 minute; add shrimp, and stir-fry 2 to 3 minutes or just until shrimp turn pink.

4. Add sauce and hot cooked noodles, tossing to coat.

ASIAN SHRIMP WITH PASTA

makes: 6 servings hands-on time: 25 min. total time: 33 min.

It may seem like a lot of ingredients, but you'll make this often, so keep these items on hand.

1	lb. unpeeled, medium-size raw shrimp
1	(9-oz.) package refrigerated angel hair pasta
¼	cup lite soy sauce
¼	cup seasoned rice wine vinegar
2	tsp. sesame oil
6	green onions, chopped
1	cup frozen sweet peas, thawed
¾	cup shredded carrots
1	(8-oz.) can sliced water chestnuts, drained
¼	cup chopped fresh cilantro
2	Tbsp. minced fresh ginger
2	garlic cloves, minced
1	tsp. vegetable oil
2	Tbsp. fresh lime juice
½	tsp. freshly ground black pepper
2	Tbsp. chopped unsalted dry-roasted peanuts

1. Peel shrimp, and devein, if desired. Set shrimp aside.

2. Prepare pasta according to package directions. Drain and place in a large bowl or on a platter.

3. Stir together soy sauce, vinegar, and sesame oil. Drizzle over pasta. Add green onions and next 4 ingredients to pasta; toss.

4. Sauté ginger and garlic in hot vegetable oil 1 to 2 minutes. (Do not brown.) Add shrimp, lime juice, and pepper; cook 3 to 5 minutes or just until shrimp turn pink. Add shrimp mixture to pasta mixture, and toss. Sprinkle with nuts. Serve immediately.

SWEET CHILI-LIME NOODLES WITH VEGETABLES

makes: 1 serving hands-on time: 10 min. total time: 15 min.

This is the perfect dish to make when you need a quick dinner for one. It also multiplies easily to serve more.

1   **cup cooked whole grain spaghetti (2 oz. uncooked)**

2   **cups shredded bok choy***

¼   **cup grated carrot**

¼   **cup fresh snow peas**

Sweet Chili-Lime Sauce

¼   **cup shredded cooked chicken (optional)**

1. Place pasta, next 4 ingredients, and, if desired, chicken in a medium-size microwave-safe plastic container. Cover with lid, and shake to combine.

2. Lift 1 corner of lid to allow steam to escape. Microwave at HIGH 2 minutes or until vegetables are tender.

* 2 cups shredded coleslaw mix or shredded cabbage may be substituted.

SWEET CHILI-LIME SAUCE

makes: about 3 Tbsp.
hands-on time: 5 min.
total time: 5 min.

2   **Tbsp. bottled sweet chili sauce**

2   **tsp. lime juice**

½   **tsp. freshly grated ginger**

¼   **tsp. minced garlic**

1. Stir together all ingredients until blended.

PORK LO-MEIN

makes: 4 servings   hands-on time: 15 min.   total time: 27 min.

If you cook the pork and vegetables in vegetable oil instead of sesame oil, this dish will have a milder flavor and fragrance.

- **8 oz. uncooked lo-mein noodles or thin spaghetti**
- **1 Tbsp. sesame oil or vegetable oil**
- **4 boneless pork loin chops (1 lb.), cut into ¼-inch strips**
- **1 small onion, sliced**
- **1 cup sliced fresh mushrooms**
- **¾ cup chopped celery (about 2 ribs)**
- **⅓ cup soy sauce**
- **¼ tsp. freshly ground black pepper**

1. Prepare noodles according to package directions. Drain well; keep warm.

2. Heat oil in a large skillet or wok over medium-high heat 2 minutes. Add pork, and stir-fry 5 minutes or until done. Remove from skillet.

3. Add onion, mushrooms, and celery to skillet; stir-fry 4 minutes. Stir in soy sauce. Return pork to skillet; stir-fry 1 minute. Stir in cooked pasta and pepper, tossing to coat. Serve immediately.

SESAME GINGER SHRIMP

makes: 4 servings   hands-on time: 20 min.   total time: 30 min.

4   oz. fresh snow peas

1   lb. peeled, large raw shrimp

1   (11-oz.) package Asian-style noodles with soy-ginger sauce

⅛   tsp. table salt

1   Tbsp. vegetable oil

2   Tbsp. lime juice

Toppings: chopped peanuts, chopped fresh cilantro

1. Trim ends and remove strings from snow peas; discard ends and strings. Devein shrimp, if desired.

2. Cook noodles according to package directions, reserving sauce and topping packets. Drain and keep warm.

3. Sprinkle shrimp with salt. Sauté shrimp in hot oil in a large nonstick skillet over high heat 2 minutes or just until shrimp turn pink. Remove shrimp from skillet, and keep warm.

4. Sauté snow peas in skillet over high heat, stirring often, 2 to 3 minutes or until tender. Return shrimp to skillet; stir in reserved sauce packet and lime juice, and cook 30 seconds. Stir in hot cooked noodles. Serve with desired toppings. Sprinkle with reserved sesame seed topping packet.

VIETNAMESE NOODLE-VEGETABLE TOSS

makes: 3 servings hands-on time: 10 min. total time: 15 min.

Vietnamese cuisine is truly light Asian food. Rice noodles make this a hearty dish without leaving you feeling overly full.

- 6 oz. uncooked linguine-style rice noodles
- 1 Tbsp. sugar
- 2 Tbsp. water
- 1 Tbsp. fish sauce
- 1 Tbsp. fresh lime juice
- 2 cups packaged tricolor slaw mix
- 1 cup grated English cucumber
- 1 cup fresh bean sprouts
- 1 cup fresh cilantro leaves
- ½ cup chopped unsalted, dry-roasted peanuts

1. Bring 6 cups water to a boil in a large saucepan. Remove from heat; add rice noodles. Let soak 3 minutes or until tender. Drain.

2. While noodles soak, combine sugar and next 3 ingredients in a small bowl, stirring well with a whisk.

3. Combine noodles, slaw mix, and next 3 ingredients in a large bowl. Toss with sugar mixture. Sprinkle with peanuts. Serve immediately.

SPICY SHRIMP NOODLE BOWL

makes: 4 servings   hands-on time: 15 min.   total time: 20 min.

Try this twist: Add additional fresh cilantro and a squeeze of lime juice for extra flavor.

1   (8.2-oz.) package teriyaki-flavored Asian-style noodles

2   (14.5-oz.) cans chicken broth

1   lb. peeled, medium-size raw shrimp, deveined

¼   cup spicy Szechuan sauce

2   cups shredded napa cabbage

1   cup fresh snow peas, trimmed and cut into 1-inch pieces

¾   cup shredded carrots

¼   cup loosely packed fresh cilantro leaves

3   green onions, thinly sliced

1. Cook noodles according to package directions; drain.

2. Stir together flavor packet from noodles and chicken broth in a 3-qt. saucepan. Bring to a boil; add shrimp, and cook 3 minutes. Stir in Szechuan sauce and next 3 ingredients. Cook 2 minutes. Stir in noodles, cilantro, and green onions.

CHICKEN CHOW MEIN

makes: 6 servings   hands-on time: 15 min.   total time: 15 min.

East meets West in this popular Asian-American dish. The chow mein method involves cooking small pieces of meat or seafood and vegetables separately, then combining and serving them atop crisp noodles.

¼	cup butter
4	cups chopped cooked chicken
1	medium onion, chopped
3	celery ribs, chopped
1	medium-size green bell pepper, chopped
2	(10¾-oz.) cans cream of mushroom soup, undiluted
¼	cup soy sauce
1	(2-oz.) jar diced pimiento, undrained
1	(5-oz.) can chow mein noodles
1	cup salted cashews
	Garnish: sliced fresh chives

1. Cook butter in a large skillet over medium-high heat, stirring often, until lightly browned. Add chicken and next 6 ingredients; cook, stirring often, 10 to 12 minutes.

2. Serve over noodles, and sprinkle with salted cashews.

Have the kids divide the chow mein noodles into six bowls before serving.

LITTLE HELPERS

Sides & More

With any great pasta
comes delicious breads, salads,
and, of course, desserts!

HERBED GOAT CHEESE TOASTS

makes: 8 servings   hands-on time: 10 min.   total time: 10 min.

½   cup crumbled goat cheese

¾   tsp. dried oregano

½   tsp. garlic powder

¼   tsp. paprika

⅛   tsp. table salt

8   (1-oz.) slices French bread

1. Preheat oven to broil. Combine first 5 ingredients; sprinkle over French bread slices. Broil for 2 minutes or until lightly browned.

OREGANO BREADSTICKS

makes: 6 to 8 servings   hands-on time: 5 min.   total time: 18 min.

1   (11-oz.) can refrigerated breadstick dough

1   Tbsp. olive oil

1   tsp. dried oregano

1. Preheat oven to 375°. Unroll dough, and brush with olive oil; sprinkle with 1 tsp. dried oregano. Separate dough into individual breadsticks, and place on a lightly greased baking sheet.

2. Bake at 375° for 13 minutes or until lightly browned.

CRUSTY ITALIAN BREAD
WITH HERBED OLIVE OIL

makes: 8 to 10 servings   hands-on time: 5 min.   total time: 5 min.

¼ **cup olive oil**

1 **tsp. dried Italian seasoning**

1 **tsp. minced garlic**

1 **(16-oz.) loaf Italian bread, sliced**

1. In a small skillet, heat olive oil; add dried Italian seasoning and minced garlic. Sauté 2 minutes. Serve in a dipping bowl with Italian bread.

Teach your kids how to mince fresh garlic with the help of a garlic press.

LITTLE HELPERS

STRAWBERRY CAPRESE BRUSCHETTA

makes: 10 to 12 servings hands-on time: 20 min. total time: 35 min.

This refreshing mixture of nectarine, grape tomatoes, strawberries, and basil are served over baguette slices with slatherings of goat cheese.

1½ cups sliced fresh strawberries

1 (10.5-oz.) goat cheese log, softened and rolled into ½-inch balls

1 nectarine, diced

1 cup quartered grape tomatoes

3 Tbsp. thinly sliced fresh basil

1 shallot, minced

2 Tbsp. olive oil

1 Tbsp. balsamic vinegar

1 tsp. sugar

1 tsp. freshly ground black pepper

¼ tsp. table salt

1 (12-oz.) French bread baguette

1. Preheat oven to 375°. Stir together strawberries, goat cheese, nectarine, grape tomatoes, basil, minced shallot, olive oil, balsamic vinegar, sugar, pepper, and salt.

2. Split baguette in half; cut each half crosswise into 4 equal pieces. Place bread pieces on a baking sheet, and bake 13 to 15 minutes or until thoroughly heated. Remove from oven, and top with strawberry mixture. Cut into 2-inch slices.

EASY THREE-SEED PAN ROLLS

makes: 9 rolls   hands-on time: 10 min.   total time: 3 hours, 25 min.

The initial cost for these rolls is money well spent. You can make three batches from one package.

- 4   tsp. fennel seeds
- 4   tsp. poppy seeds
- 4   tsp. sesame seeds
- 9   frozen bread dough rolls
- 1   large egg white, beaten

Melted butter

1. Combine first 3 ingredients in a small bowl. Dip dough rolls, 1 at a time, in egg white; roll in seed mixture. Arrange rolls, 1 inch apart, in a lightly greased 8-inch pan. Cover with lightly greased plastic wrap, and let rise in a warm place (80° to 85°), free from drafts, 3 to 4 hours or until doubled in bulk.

2. Preheat oven to 350°. Uncover rolls, and bake at 350° for 15 minutes or until golden. Brush with melted butter.

Three-Seed French Bread:
Substitute 1 (11-oz.) can refrigerated French bread dough for frozen bread dough rolls. Combine seeds in a shallow dish. Brush dough loaf with egg white. Roll top and sides of dough loaf in seeds. Place, seam side down, on a baking sheet. Cut and bake dough loaf according to package directions.

HURRY-UP HOMEMADE CRESCENT ROLLS

makes: 1 dozen   hands-on time: 25 min.   total time: 1 hour, 35 min.

The title says it all—yummy, fragrant rolls that call for just a few ingredients and minimal effort.

1	(¼-oz.) envelope active dry yeast
¾	cup warm water (105° to 115°)
3	to 3½ cups all-purpose baking mix
2	Tbsp. sugar

Think ahead and freeze rolls up to two months. Bake at 425° for 5 minutes; cool completely (about 30 minutes). Wrap in aluminum foil, and freeze in an airtight container. Thaw at room temperature on a lightly greased baking sheet; bake at 425° for 7 to 8 minutes or until golden.

1. Combine yeast and warm water in a 1-cup measuring cup; let stand 5 minutes. Combine 3 cups baking mix and sugar in a large bowl; gradually stir in yeast mixture.

2. Turn dough out onto a floured surface, and knead, adding additional baking mix (up to ½ cup) as needed, until dough is smooth and elastic (about 10 minutes).

3. Roll dough into a 12-inch circle; cut circle into 12 wedges. Roll up wedges, starting at wide end, to form a crescent shape; place, point sides down, on a lightly greased baking sheet. Cover and let rise in a warm place (80° to 85°), free from drafts, 1 hour or until doubled in bulk.

4. Preheat oven to 425°. Bake 10 to 12 minutes or until golden.

Note: To make rolls in a heavy-duty electric stand mixer, prepare as directed in Step 1. Beat dough at medium speed, using dough hook attachment, about 5 minutes, beating in ½ cup additional baking mix, if needed, until dough leaves the sides of the bowl and pulls together, becoming soft and smooth. Proceed with recipe as directed in Step 3. We tested with Bisquick® Original Pancake and Baking Mix.

ROMAINE SALAD

makes: 8 servings hands-on time: 5 min. total time: 5 min.

¼ cup mayonnaise

2 Tbsp. Dijon mustard

4 tsp. fresh lemon juice

2 tsp. red wine vinegar

4 garlic cloves, minced

16 cups torn romaine lettuce

Garnishes: freshly grated Parmesan cheese, freshly ground black pepper

1. In a large bowl, whisk together first 5 ingredients. Add romaine lettuce, tossing gently to coat.

Little Helpers

Place the dressing in an airtight container and let the kids shake it until the dressing comes together.

GOURMET GREENS
WITH ORANGES AND RAISINS

makes: 6 servings hands-on time: 5 min. total time: 5 min.

1½ **cups gourmet mixed salad greens**

2 **cups mandarin orange slices**

¾ **cup golden raisins**

Bottled balsamic vinaigrette

1. Arrange salad greens on each of 6 plates. Top each serving with ⅓ cup mandarin orange slices and 2 Tbsp. golden raisins. Drizzle each serving with bottled balsamic vinaigrette. Serve immediately.

To make your own vinaigrette, mix ¼ cup balsamic vinegar, ⅔ cup olive oil, and table salt and freshly ground black pepper to taste until well combined.

PASTA POINTER

MEDITERRANEAN PANZANELLA SALAD

makes: 4 servings hands-on time: 10 min. total time: 15 min.

Like many Italian dishes, panzanella (pahn-zah-NEHL-lah) was probably first made out of necessity—combining stale bread with readily available fresh garden vegetables. For added color, we chose to use a combination of yellow and red heirloom tomatoes.

1	Tbsp. vegetable oil
3	Tbsp. white balsamic vinegar
⅛	tsp. table salt
¼	tsp. freshly ground black pepper
6½	cups chopped tomato (3 very large)
1½	cups cubed English cucumber
½	cup pitted kalamata olives
½	cup fresh basil leaves, torn
6	oz. whole wheat country-style bread, torn into bite-size pieces (4 cups)
1	(4-oz.) package crumbled feta cheese

1. Combine first 4 ingredients in a large bowl, stirring with a whisk. Stir in tomato and next 3 ingredients. Add bread and cheese; toss gently. Serve immediately.

PASTA POINTER

If you prefer a drier panzanella, toast the bread before tossing it with the tomato mixture.

ITALIAN SALAD

makes: 8 servings   hands-on time: 15 min.   total time: 15 min.

No need to cook the frozen artichoke hearts—just thaw, and pat dry.

1   head iceberg lettuce (about 1 lb.), torn

1   (9-oz.) package frozen artichoke hearts, thawed*

1   (2.25-oz.) can sliced black olives, drained

1   small red bell pepper, chopped

1¼ cups large-cut croutons

½   cup sliced pepperoncini salad peppers

¼   cup chopped red onion

¾   cup refrigerated creamy Asiago-peppercorn or Parmesan-peppercorn dressing

Cracked black pepper (optional)

1. Place lettuce in a 4-qt. bowl. Arrange artichoke hearts and next 5 ingredients over lettuce. Top with dressing; gently toss to combine. Sprinkle with cracked black pepper, if desired. Serve immediately.

* 1 (14-oz.) can artichoke hearts, drained, may be substituted.

TOMATO-CUCUMBER SALAD

makes: 4 servings hands-on time: 10 min. total time: 10 min.

Chill out on hot summer days with the fresh flavors of this cool, crisp salad.

1	seedless cucumber, sliced
½	small onion, thinly sliced
2	cups small, vine-ripened tomatoes, cut into quarters*
¼	cup olive oil-and-vinegar dressing
½	tsp. lemon zest
1	Tbsp. lemon juice
	Chopped fresh parsley

1. Stir together cucumber, onion, and tomatoes. Add oil-and-vinegar dressing, lemon zest, lemon juice, parsley, and table salt and freshly ground black pepper to taste. Toss to coat.

* 2 cups grape or cherry tomatoes, halved, may be substituted.

FETA-STUFFED TOMATOES

makes: 8 servings   hands-on time: 15 min.   total time: 30 min.

4   **large tomatoes**

4   **oz. crumbled feta cheese**

¼   **cup fine, dry breadcrumbs**

2   **Tbsp. chopped green onions**

2   **Tbsp. chopped fresh parsley**

2   **Tbsp. olive oil**

Garnish: chopped fresh parsley

1. Preheat oven to 350°. Cut 4 large tomatoes in half horizontally. Scoop out pulp from each tomato half, leaving shells intact; discard seeds, and coarsely chop pulp. Stir together pulp, feta cheese, dry breadcrumbs, green onions, parsley, and olive oil in a medium bowl. Spoon mixture evenly into tomato shells, and place in a 13- x 9-inch baking dish. Bake at 350° for 15 minutes.

DRESSED-UP CHOPPED CAESAR SALAD

makes: 4 servings hands-on time: 25 min. total time: 30 min.

These flavorful croutons are made in the microwave.

- 2 **Tbsp. butter**
- 1 **garlic clove, minced**
- 4 **pumpernickel bread slices, cut into 1-inch cubes**
- 2 **romaine lettuce hearts, chopped**
- 3 **cups chopped cooked turkey breast**
- 1 **pt. cherry tomatoes, cut in half**
- 4 **oz. Asiago cheese, cut into small cubes**
- 4 **thick bacon slices, cooked and crumbled**
- 2 **green onions, thinly sliced**
- ½ **cup bottled creamy Caesar dressing**

1. Microwave butter in a microwave-safe pie plate at HIGH 30 seconds or until melted. Stir in garlic, and microwave 45 seconds or until fragrant. Stir in bread cubes and desired amounts of table salt and freshly ground black pepper. Microwave at HIGH 4 minutes or until crisp, stirring at 1-minute intervals. Cool 5 minutes.

2. Toss together romaine lettuce and next 5 ingredients. Drizzle with dressing; toss gently. Sprinkle with croutons.

CRISPY SESAME SALAD STACK

makes: 6 servings hands-on time: 15 min. total time: 20 min.

Wonton wrappers can be found in the refrigerated section of most supermarkets.

1 (8-oz.) package mixed salad greens

Sesame Wonton Crisps

1 (11-oz.) can mandarin oranges, drained

2 green onions, sliced

6 Tbsp. chopped cashews

Fresh Orange-Soy Vinaigrette

1. Layer ½ cup salad greens, 1 Sesame Wonton Crisp, 3 Tbsp. salad greens, 1 Sesame Wonton Crisp, and 1 Tbsp. salad greens on a serving plate. Carefully tuck 1 Tbsp. mandarin oranges into salad greens. Repeat procedure with remaining salad greens, wonton crisps, and oranges. Sprinkle with green onions and cashews. Drizzle with Fresh Orange-Soy Vinaigrette. Add table salt and freshly ground black pepper to taste. Serve immediately.

SESAME WONTON CRISPS

makes: 1 dozen hands-on time: 5 min. total time: 10 min.

12 wonton wrappers

1 Tbsp. melted butter

½ tsp. white sesame seeds

½ tsp. black sesame seeds

¼ tsp. kosher salt

1. Preheat oven to 425°. Place wonton wrappers on an ungreased baking sheet. Brush 1 side of each wrapper with melted butter; sprinkle with sesame seeds and salt.

2. Bake at 425° for 5 to 6 minutes or until golden brown.

FRESH ORANGE-SOY VINAIGRETTE

makes: about ½ cup
hands-on time: 10 min.
total time: 10 min.

¼ cup rice vinegar

¼ cup orange juice

2 Tbsp. vegetable oil

1 Tbsp. soy sauce

2 Tbsp. dark brown sugar

1 tsp. freshly grated ginger

⅛ tsp. dry mustard

1. Combine rice vinegar and next 6 ingredients in a food processor; pulse 3 or 4 times or until smooth. Add table salt to taste.

SPINACH SALAD
WITH HONEY DRESSING AND HONEYED PECANS

makes: 6 to 8 servings hands-on time: 15 min. total time: 45 min.

Use leftover dressing to marinate meat.

- 1 (6-oz.) package fresh baby spinach
- 1 cup quartered fresh strawberries
- ½ cup thinly sliced red onion
- ½ cup fresh blueberries
- Honey Dressing
- 3 to 4 cooked bacon slices, crumbled
- ¼ cup crumbled blue cheese
- Honeyed Pecans

1. Toss together first 4 ingredients and ⅓ cup dressing. Sprinkle with bacon, cheese, and pecans. Serve with remaining dressing.

HONEY DRESSING

makes: about 1 cup hands-on time: 5 min. total time: 5 min.

- ⅓ cup white balsamic vinegar
- 2 Tbsp. honey
- 1 Tbsp. Dijon mustard
- ½ tsp. table salt
- ½ tsp. freshly ground black pepper
- ⅔ cup extra virgin olive oil

1. Whisk together vinegar and next 4 ingredients. Add oil in a slow, steady stream, whisking constantly until smooth.

HONEYED PECANS

makes: 1 cup
hands-on time: 10 min.
total time: 25 min.

- ¼ cup honey
- 1 cup pecan halves
- Parchment paper
- 1 Tbsp. sugar
- ¼ tsp. kosher salt
- Pinch of ground red pepper

1. Preheat oven to 325°. Microwave honey in a microwave-safe bowl at HIGH 20 seconds. Stir in pecan halves. Coat a parchment paper-lined jelly-roll pan with cooking spray; spread pecans in a single layer on pan. Combine sugar, salt, and a pinch of ground red pepper; sprinkle over pecans. Bake at 325° for 15 minutes or until toasted, stirring after 8 minutes. Cool completely; break into pieces.

LEMON MELTAWAYS

makes: about 3½ dozen hands-on time: 30 min. total time: 2 hours

These tangy, citrusy, and delicate little gems are pure bliss. They get their melt-in-your-mouth flavor from lots of butter, lemon juice, and zest.

- ¾ **cup plus 2 Tbsp. butter, softened**
- 1½ **cups powdered sugar, divided**
- 1 **Tbsp. loosely packed lemon zest**
- 2 **Tbsp. fresh lemon juice**
- 1½ **cups all-purpose flour**
- ¼ **cup cornstarch**
- ¼ **tsp. table salt**
- **Parchment paper**

1. Beat butter at medium speed with a heavy-duty electric stand mixer until creamy. Add ½ cup powdered sugar; beat at medium speed until light and fluffy. Stir in zest and juice. Whisk together flour and next 2 ingredients. Gradually add flour mixture to butter mixture, beating at low speed just until blended. Cover and chill 1 hour.

2. Preheat oven to 350°. Drop dough by level spoonfuls 2 inches apart onto parchment paper-lined baking sheets, using a 1-inch cookie scoop.

3. Bake at 350° for 13 minutes or until lightly browned around edges. Cool on baking sheets 5 minutes.

4. Toss together warm cookies and remaining 1 cup powdered sugar in a small bowl.

Soften butter quickly by cutting it into small pieces and placing it in a single layer on a plate.

Speed It Up!

RASPBERRY TIRAMISÙ BITES

makes: 8 servings   hands-on time: 30 min.   total time: 2 hours, 30 min.

There are crisp Italian cookies also called ladyfingers, but be sure to use soft ones in this recipe. Look for them in the bakery or produce section of your supermarket.

3   Tbsp. seedless raspberry preserves

1   Tbsp. orange liqueur

1   (3-oz.) package cream cheese, softened

¼   cup sugar

½   cup heavy cream

8   ladyfingers, halved crosswise

8   fresh raspberries

Garnish: fresh mint sprigs

1. Microwave raspberry preserves in a small microwave-safe bowl at HIGH 20 seconds. Stir in liqueur.

2. Beat cream cheese and sugar at medium speed with an electric mixer until creamy (about 1 minute).

3. Beat heavy cream at medium-high speed with an electric mixer until soft peaks form. Fold into cream cheese mixture. Spoon into a zip-top plastic bag. (Do not seal.) Snip 1 corner of bag to make a hole (about ½ inch in diameter).

4. Press 1 ladyfinger half onto bottom of 1 (1½-oz.) shot glass. Repeat layers in 7 more shot glasses. Drizzle about ½ tsp. raspberry mixture into each glass. Pipe a small amount of cream cheese mixture evenly into each glass. Repeat layers with remaining ladyfingers, raspberry mixture, and cream cheese mixture. Top each glass with 1 raspberry. Cover and chill 2 hours.

DOUBLE COFFEE TIRAMISÙ

makes: 8 servings   hands-on time: 25 min.   total time: 2 hours, 25 min.

Coffee liqueur adds extra kick to this make-ahead Italian trifle dessert.

1 **(8-oz.) package cream cheese**

½ **cup sugar**

2 **cups whipping cream**

½ **cup hot water**

1 **Tbsp. instant coffee granules**

¼ **cup coffee liqueur**

2 **(3-oz.) packages ladyfingers**

½ **cup grated semisweet or dark chocolate**

1. Beat cream cheese and sugar at medium speed with an electric mixer until creamy.

2. Beat whipping cream with an electric mixer until soft peaks form. Fold into cream cheese mixture.

3. Stir together ½ cup hot water and coffee granules until dissolved. Stir in ¼ cup liqueur.

4. Arrange ladyfingers evenly around sides of 8 (6-oz.) coffee cups or ramekins. Drizzle ladyfingers with coffee mixture. Spoon or pipe cream cheese mixture into center of ramekins. Sprinkle with grated chocolate. Cover and chill 2 hours.

Note: To serve the tiramisù in a single dish, prepare recipe as directed through Step 3. Arrange half of ladyfingers in bottom and up sides of a 2-qt. serving bowl. Drizzle evenly with half of coffee mixture. Top with half of cream cheese mixture. Repeat layers. Sprinkle with chocolate curls. Cover and chill 2 hours.

ESPRESSO SHORTBREAD COOKIES

makes: about 4 dozen hands-on time: 45 min. total time: 3 hours, 15 min.

If you're a true coffee connoisseur or enjoy the taste of coffee revved up with chocolate, you'll enjoy these espresso-laced cookies.

- 1 **cup butter, softened**
- ½ **cup granulated sugar**
- 1 **tsp. sea salt**
- 1 **tsp. vanilla extract**
- 2 **cups all-purpose flour**
- ½ **cup chocolate-covered espresso beans, chopped**
- 1 **Tbsp. finely ground espresso beans**

Wax paper

- ½ **cup Demerara or turbinado sugar, divided**

1. Beat first 3 ingredients at medium speed with a heavy-duty electric stand mixer 2 to 3 minutes or until light and fluffy. Stir in vanilla.

2. Stir together flour and next 2 ingredients in a medium bowl. Gradually add to butter mixture, beating just until blended; stop to scrape bowl as needed. (Do not overmix.)

3. Divide dough in half. Turn 1 dough portion out onto wax paper, and shape into a 10- x 2-inch log. Sprinkle log with 3 Tbsp. Demerara sugar, and roll log back and forth to adhere. Repeat with remaining dough portion and 3 Tbsp. Demerara sugar. Wrap logs in plastic wrap, and chill 2 to 3 hours.

4. Preheat oven to 350°. Cut chilled dough into ¼-inch-thick slices, and place 1 inch apart on 2 lightly greased baking sheets. Sprinkle 1½ tsp. Demerara sugar over cookies on each sheet.

5. Bake at 350° for 12 to 15 minutes or until golden around edges, switching baking sheets halfway through.

6. Cool on baking sheets 2 to 3 minutes. Transfer to wire racks; cool 5 minutes. Serve immediately, or cool completely. Store up to 4 days.

PIÑA COLADA ICEBOX PIE

makes: 8 servings hands-on time: 25 min. total time: 6 hours, 20 min.

Press the crumb mixture all the way up the sides of the pie plate before baking; otherwise, you'll end up with a thick, uneven crust that's too shallow to hold the filling.

- **2 cups pecan shortbread cookie crumbs (about 16 cookies)**
- **1 cup sweetened flaked coconut**
- **¼ cup butter, melted**
- **⅓ cup sugar**
- **2 Tbsp. cornstarch**
- **1 (8-oz.) can crushed pineapple in juice**
- **1 (8-oz.) package cream cheese, softened**
- **1½ cups cream of coconut, divided**
- **2 large eggs**
- **1 cup whipping cream**
- **Garnishes: lightly toasted shaved coconut, pineapple wedges, fresh pineapple mint sprigs**

1. Preheat oven to 350°. Stir together first 3 ingredients; firmly press on bottom and up sides of a lightly greased 9-inch pie plate. Bake 10 to 12 minutes or until lightly browned. Transfer to a wire rack; cool completely (about 30 minutes).

2. Stir together sugar and cornstarch in a small heavy saucepan; stir in pineapple. Bring to a boil over medium-high heat, stirring constantly; cook, stirring constantly, 1 minute or until thickened. Remove from heat; cool completely (about 20 minutes).

3. Beat cream cheese at medium speed with a heavy-duty electric stand mixer, using whisk attachment, until smooth. Gradually add 1 cup cream of coconut, beating at low speed just until blended. (Chill remaining ½ cup cream of coconut until ready to use.) Add eggs, 1 at a time, beating just until blended after each addition.

4. Spread cooled pineapple mixture over bottom of piecrust; spoon cream cheese mixture over pineapple mixture.

5. Bake at 350° for 38 to 42 minutes or until set. Cool completely on a wire rack (about 1 hour). Cover and chill 4 hours.

6. Beat whipping cream at high speed with an electric mixer until foamy. Gradually add remaining ½ cup cream of coconut, beating until soft peaks form; spread over pie.

METRIC EQUIVALENTS

The information in the following charts is provided to help cooks outside the United States successfully use the recipes in this book. All equivalents are approximate.

Equivalents for Different Types of Ingredients

Standard Cup	Fine Powder (ex. flour)	Grain (ex. rice)	Granular (ex. sugar)	Liquid Solids (ex. butter)	Liquid (ex. milk)
1	140 g	150 g	190 g	200 g	240 ml
¾	105 g	113 g	143 g	150 g	180 ml
⅔	93 g	100 g	125 g	133 g	160 ml
½	70 g	75 g	95 g	100 g	120 ml
⅓	47 g	50 g	63 g	67 g	80 ml
¼	35 g	38 g	48 g	50 g	60 ml
⅛	18 g	19 g	24 g	25 g	30 ml

Liquid Ingredients by Volume

¼ tsp	=			1 ml
½ tsp	=			2 ml
1 tsp	=			5 ml
3 tsp	= 1 Tbsp =	½ fl oz	=	15 ml
2 Tbsp	= ⅛ cup =	1 fl oz	=	30 ml
4 Tbsp	= ¼ cup =	2 fl oz	=	60 ml
5⅓ Tbsp	= ⅓ cup =	3 fl oz	=	80 ml
8 Tbsp	= ½ cup =	4 fl oz	=	120 ml
10⅔ Tbsp	= ⅔ cup =	5 fl oz	=	160 ml
12 Tbsp	= ¾ cup =	6 fl oz	=	180 ml
16 Tbsp	= 1 cup =	8 fl oz	=	240 ml
1 pt	= 2 cups =	16 fl oz	=	480 ml
1 qt	= 4 cups =	32 fl oz	=	960 ml
		33 fl oz	= 1000 ml	= 1 l

Dry Ingredients by Weight

(To convert ounces to grams, multiply the number of ounces by 30.)

1 oz	=	¹⁄₁₆ lb	=	30 g
4 oz	=	¼ lb	=	120 g
8 oz	=	½ lb	=	240 g
12 oz	=	¾ lb	=	360 g
16 oz	=	1 lb	=	480 g

Length

(To convert inches to centimeters, multiply the number of inches by 2.5.)

1 in	=			2.5 cm
6 in	= ½ ft		=	15 cm
12 in	= 1 ft		=	30 cm
36 in	= 3 ft	= 1 yd	=	90 cm
40 in			=	100 cm = 1 m

Cooking/Oven Temperatures

	Fahrenheit	Celsius	Gas Mark
Freeze Water	32° F	0° C	
Room Temp.	68° F	20° C	
Boil Water	212° F	100° C	
Bake	325° F	160° C	3
	350° F	180° C	4
	375° F	190° C	5
	400° F	200° C	6
	425° F	220° C	7
	450° F	230° C	8
Broil			Grill

INDEX

ISBN-13: 978-0-8487-4369-7
ISBN-10: 0-8487-4369-5
Library of Congress Control Number: 2014940868

Printed in the United States of America
First Printing 2014

Oxmoor House
Editorial Director: Leah McLaughlin
Creative Director: Felicity Keane
Art Director: Christopher Rhoads
Executive Food Director: Grace Parisi
Senior Editor: Rebecca Brennan
Managing Editor: Elizabeth Tyler Austin
Assistant Managing Editor: Jeanne de Lathouder

Pasta Night!
Editors: Meredith Butcher, Allison E. Cox
Assistant Designer: Allison Sperando Potter
Assistant Test Kitchen Manager:
   Alyson Moreland Haynes
Recipe Developers and Testers: Wendy Ball, R.D.;
   Tamara Goldis, R.D.; Stefanie Maloney; Callie Nash;
   Karen Rankin; Leah Van Deren
Food Stylists: Victoria E. Cox, Margaret Monroe Dickey,
   Catherine Crowell Steele
Photography Director: Jim Bathie
Senior Photographer: Hélène Dujardin
Senior Photo Stylist: Kay E. Clarke
Photo Stylist: Mindi Shapiro Levine
Assistant Photo Stylist: Mary Louise Menendez
Senior Production Managers: Greg A. Amason,
   Susan Chodakiewicz

Contributors
Project Editor: Sarah Waller
Copy Editor: Donna Baldone
Proofreader: Lauren Brooks
Indexer: Nanette Cardon
Fellows: Ali Carruba, Kylie Dazzo, Elizabeth Laseter,
   Madison Taylor Pozzo, Anna Ramia, Deanna Sakal,
   April Smitherman, Tonya West
Photographer: Johnny Autry
Food and Photo Stylist: Charlotte Autry

Time Home Entertainment Inc.
President and Publisher: Jim Childs
Vice President and Assoicate Publisher:
Margot Schupf
Vice President, Finance: Vandana Patel
Executive Director, Marketing Services: Carol Pittard
Executive Publishing Director: Joy Butts
Publishing Director: Megan Pearlman
Associate General Counsel: Simone Procas